AMAZING BUT TRUE!

Written by Elizabeth Dowsett, Julia March, and Catherine Saunders

AMAZING BUT TRUE!

Fun Facts about the LEGO® World—and our own!

Contents

CHAPTER 1

Nature

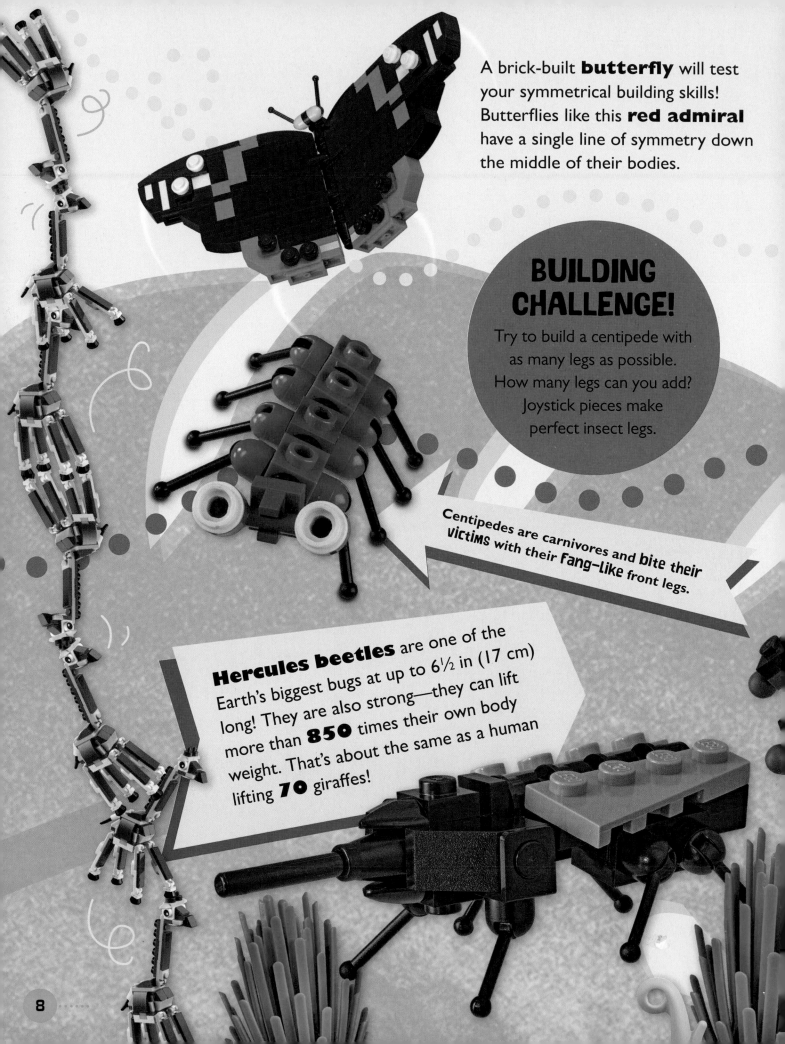

A brick-built **butterfly** will test your symmetrical building skills! Butterflies like this **red admiral** have a single line of symmetry down the middle of their bodies.

BUILDING CHALLENGE!

Try to build a centipede with as many legs as possible. How many legs can you add? Joystick pieces make perfect insect legs.

Centipedes are carnivores and bite their **victims** with their **fang-like** front legs.

Hercules beetles are one of the Earth's biggest bugs at up to 6½ in (17 cm) long! They are also strong—they can lift more than **850** times their own body weight. That's about the same as a human lifting **70** giraffes!

How many LEGO® bricks does a Goliath spider weigh?

The world's heaviest spider is the **Goliath tarantula**. It weighs up to 6 oz (175 g)—the equivalent of **75** 2x4 LEGO® bricks. Try holding 75 bricks in your hands all at once and pretend you're holding a Goliath!

Why does a **snail** make **slime?** It helps it move and keeps its body protected from bumpy surfaces. Create your own LEGO snail slime with a trail of transparent tile pieces.

Ladybugs are the best—don't bug me about it!

A Goliath spider could cover a dinner plate with its long, bristly legs!

10 insect- and spider-themed Collectible LEGO Minifigure Series have been released, including **Ladybug Girl**, **Butterfly Girl**, and the **Beekeeper**.

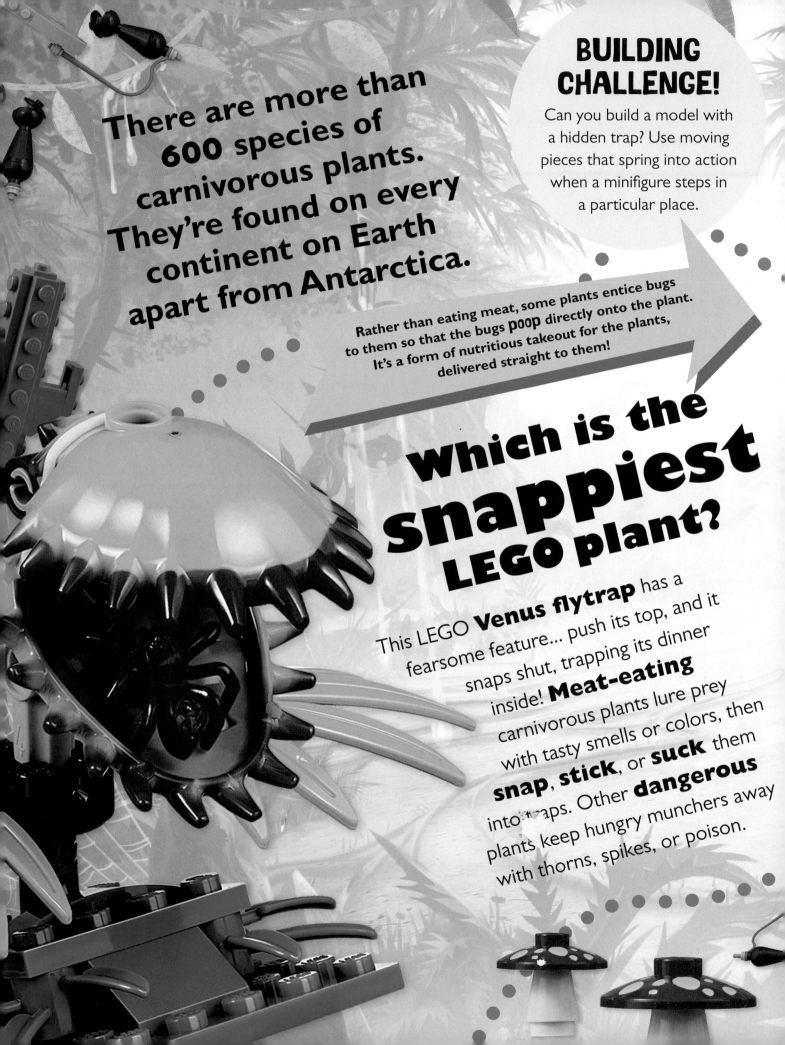

There are more than **600 species of carnivorous plants.** They're found on every continent on Earth apart from Antarctica.

BUILDING CHALLENGE!
Can you build a model with a hidden trap? Use moving pieces that spring into action when a minifigure steps in a particular place.

Rather than eating meat, some plants entice bugs to them so that the bugs **poop** directly onto the plant. It's a form of nutritious takeout for the plants, delivered straight to them!

which is the snappiest LEGO plant?

This LEGO **Venus flytrap** has a fearsome feature... push its top, and it snaps shut, trapping its dinner inside! **Meat-eating** carnivorous plants lure prey with tasty smells or colors, then **snap**, **stick**, or **suck** them into traps. Other **dangerous** plants keep hungry munchers away with thorns, spikes, or poison.

LEGO® NEXO KNIGHTS™ hero Macy Halbert has **dangerous** plants on her side in Ultimate Macy (70331). She uses **Jungle Dragon vines** to **tangle up** the Lava.

FEED me!

Ouch! Spines help keep cacti cool in the desert and put off **predators**. This LEGO cactus is built around a central pillar so that LEGO studs face outward and create the texture of **spines**.

The **smooth** surface of the LEGO pitchers on this carnivorous **pitcher plant** is just like the real thing—so slippery that creatures slide into the **lethal liquid** at the bottom of the cups and can't crawl out.

Thanks to a LEGO® Technic spinning function, these **Whirling Vines** (70109) from the LEGO® Legends of Chima™ theme really **whoosh**. Gorzan the gorilla must dodge the deadly vines and sharp fangs of this carnivorous plant to complete the Speedorz challenge and win magical CHI energy.

Meat-eating tropical pitcher plants can grow more than **4 ft** (**120 cm**) tall. The biggest have been known to eat small **rats**, **birds**, and **frogs**.

Which LEGO fish glows 'n the dark?

The **anglerfish** from Ocean Exploration Submarine (60264) is made with glow-in-the-dark materials. This is because, deep in the dark ocean, the female anglerfish **lures** prey by emitting bioluminescent light from a **spine above her mouth**. It can be dangerous in the ocean...

Glow-in-the-dark **LEGO** bricks are **phosphorescent**: they slowly emit light that they've absorbed during the day from the sun or electric light bulbs. Glow-in-the-dark creatures are **bioluminescent**: chemical reactions in their bodies produce light.

The toothy LEGO anglerfish shoots out of its cave on a clear LEGO® Technic brick. Anglerfish bodies are so stretchy and their mouths so massive that they can swallow prey twice their size.

The first LEGO glow-in-the-dark piece was created in 1990. It was a spooky glowing shroud for a ghost minifigure.

This ferocious **fangtooth** has individual LEGO teeth and red spikes. Fangtooths look as fierce as anglerfish, but they are only about 6 in (15 cm) long.

A mix of curved and sloped bricks make this ax-head-shaped hatchet fish. The deep-sea fish emits light to hide itself. Special light organs on its underside shine down so predators below it don't see its shadows against the sunlight.

Octopus tentacles each have their own **mini-brain** so they think and act independently. This LEGO octopus has two sets of four curling tentacles connected with a **turntable** piece so they can also do their own thing.

Something fishy's going on...

BUILDING CHALLENGE!

Build a wall of transparent bricks, then make an underwater scene behind it. What lurks in the water? Has anything unusual drifted in?

T. rex is the star of the **LEGO® Jurassic World** dinosaur theme, which began in 2015.

A real *Tyrannosaurus rex* **fossilized skeleton** in the American Museum of Natural History has **terrifying teeth** more than 6 in (15 cm) long—that's the combined height of almost four minifigures per tooth!

I love eggsploring.

How long is a LEGO dinosaur fossil?

The **longest** LEGO dinosaur fossil is the *Tyrannosaurus rex*, which measures 15⅓ in (39 cm)—**32** times smaller than the real thing. It comes in the LEGO® Ideas set Dinosaur Fossils (21320), along with the skeletons of a Triceratops and a Pteranodon.

Pteranodon aren't actually dinosaurs, but they did live at the same time. They belong to a group of **flying** creatures called **pterosaurs**.

Skeleton building often uses hinged bricks for bendable hips, knees, and ankles. Can you use hinged bricks to create joints in your dino builds?

Fossilized LEGO figure "**LEGO sapiens**" is a classic skeleton with a fedora—as worn by the most famous archaeologist minifigure of all time, **Indiana Jones.**

LEGO SAPIENS

Unlike a real *Triceratops*, this LEGO version has a **frill** made of many elements rather than a single piece. It does have the **three horns** that gives the creature its name.

I'm working my fingers to the bone.

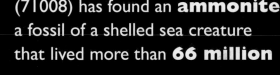

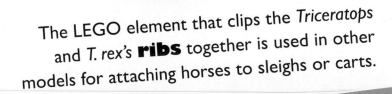

The LEGO element that clips the *Triceratops* and *T. rex*'s **ribs** together is used in other models for attaching horses to sleighs or carts.

The paleontologist from the Collectible LEGO Minifigure Series (71008) has found an **ammonite**— a fossil of a shelled sea creature that lived more than **66 million** years ago.

Which LEGO flower comes from the biggest family?

Orchids are the largest family of flowers, with more than **25,000** species. That's more than mammals and birds combined! With their **enticing** colors and fragrances, flowers are the crucial part of a plant that attracts insects and other pollinators.

This orchid's **petal** piece has appeared in LEGO sets as a **shell**, a **treasure chest**, a bird's plumage, the base of a fountain, **monstrous jaws**, a sink, a **skeleton pirate's** mouth, armor, a boat canopy, and the prow of a ship.

Most orchid flowers **grow upside down** because of the weight of their blooms.

gold crown

robot head

car hood

car roof

Busy bees, insects, birds, and bats spread pollen from flower to flower. This enables plants to make seeds to grow new plants, including a lot of our food. Without pollination, we would have no **chips** or **chocolate**!

These elegant LEGO roses (40460) have no thorns—nor do any roses. The spiky parts are actually "**prickles.**" Prickles and thorns are separate things because they're made from different parts of a plant.

The Guinness World Record for the **longest daisy chain** is 1 ⅓ miles (2.12 km.) That's longer than **94 thousand** minifigures holding hands! The record for the longest LEGO daisy chain is still up for grabs...

Water lilies float on the surface of the water, supported by a network of underwater stems. The world's largest **lily pads** grow up to **10 ft (3 m)** across and a single one can hold up to **143 lb (65 kg)**— that's the weight of a small person or more than **28,000** 2x4 LEGO bricks!

Blooming marvellous!

BUILDING CHALLENGE!

Brighten up someone's day with a gift of brick-built flowers. Experiment with colors, textures, and shapes to create a variety of organic forms.

Three dusky-pink **roses**, **lavender** sprigs, daisies, an orange California **poppy**, **snap-dragons**, and a purple **aster** make up this **never-wilting Flower Bouquet** (10280). The flowers use some unexpected LEGO elements.

Where is the best place for LEGO bird watching?

Calling all **bird watchers**! Outback Cabin (31098) is the ideal place for watching birds. After a day of watching wildlife, rebuild the LEGO® Creator 3-in-1 set into a log cabin for a good night's sleep, then a canal boat to journey to another location. There are so many birds to watch on Earth, from **ducks** in the park to **penguins** in Antarctica.

Bald eagles sound bald from their name, and they may look it from a distance —but their heads are crowned with **snowy white feathers**. This eagle from the Outback Cabin set is topped with a round, white plate.

The **albatross** is the biggest seabird, with a **wing span** reaching **11 ft** (3.35 m.) That's almost as long as 20 of these albatross models.

The first molded **LEGO bird** hatched in 1989 as a parrot in the Pirates theme. It's since spread its wings in more than **10 colors** and has been spotted across many themes, including in 2009 as a **dual-molded** red-and-green parrot.

BUILDING CHALLENGE!

Challenge your friends to build a duck from simple pieces. Don't peep until you're done. How many different types of duck do you have?

What came first, the LEGO chicken or the LEGO egg?

The chicken! This single-molded chicken piece came in **2011** with the LEGO® Kingdoms theme, then **2016** saw the arrival of this egg, initially in the LEGO® *The Angry Birds Movie*™ theme. Fried eggs arrived in **2018**.

This brick-built condor has hinges to move its wings, though real condors rarely flap theirs. They **glide** by riding air currents, sometimes going five hours without flapping.

Say — "Freeze!"

Blue-footed boobies from the Galapagos Islands really do have legs and feet as blue as these LEGO pieces. The male birds wave their **blue feet** in the air in an elaborate mating dance.

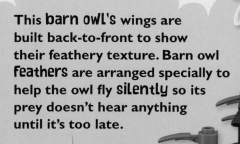

This **barn owl's** wings are built back-to-front to show their feathery texture. Barn owl **feathers** are arranged specially to help the owl fly **silently** so its prey doesn't hear anything until it's too late.

Which LEGO animal has a **surprise sting?**

Male **platypuses** have **spurs** on their back legs for injecting their rivals with poison. Other animals also use **toxic chemicals** to disable their prey, beat rivals, or defend themselves. Watch out for **teeth, stingers,** and **tentacles!**

BUILDING CHALLENGE!

Try speed building strange alien creatures with venomous features. How many different combinations can you make? Colored transparent pieces look very toxic!

As part of the LEGO® Galaxy Squad theme, **Warp Stinger (70702)** is an insect-inspired vehicle of an invading mosquitoid alien. Two cockpit covers look like giant, glowing **bug eyes** and it delivers **stinging blows** from its curved tail and long mosquito-like proboscis.

My honey is the bee's knees!

This cute Collectible LEGO Minifigure Series Bumblebee Girl is all insect, with wings and antenna, but she doesn't have a sting in her tail.

Even if this scorpion's articulated **stinging tail** doesn't get you, there are still **pincers** and its sharp **bite** to evade. The creature from LEGO Creator 3-in-1 Fire Dragon (31102) can be rebuilt as a fire-breathing dragon or a snarling saber-tooth tiger.

The swishing tail of the spotted eagle ray comes with barbed stingers.

Clear transparent bricks make up the jellylike bulk of this **purple** **stinger jellyfish.** Even after its **stinger jellyfish.** Even after its body is dead, its **stinging cells** can still hurt you!

LEGO Technic pins in yellow macaroni tubes capture these **blue rings** that appear when the blue-ringed octopus feels threatened. Its super-strength **blue rings** that appear when threatened. Its super-strength poison is especially the octopus but fortunately **deadly.** It's super-deadly, the blue-ringed octopus. Its super-strength poison is especially the octopus but fortunately isn't aggressive.

— Minifigures can't be stung, right?

Not all stingers are harmful to everyone. The clownfish prospers among the **stinging tentacles** of the **sea anemone,** where it's protected from predators who aren't so lucky. In turn, the clownfish gives the anemone nutrients and scares off predators.

Woof woof!

Which LEGO animal saves the day?

Dogs are everyday **super heroes**. Four-legged friends bring fun and joy, but also **life-saving** super skills. Heroic hounds help out in many LEGO® City sets alongside the police, coastguard, the fire service, and Arctic explorers.

Police dogs like this one in Police Dog Unit (60241) **sniff out** stolen goods, like these gems. No human-made machine can yet beat a dog's super sense of smell!

Search and rescue dogs work alongside the fire service like this one in Fire Station (60215). Fire investigation dogs even help **solve** how fires start and whether they're crimes.

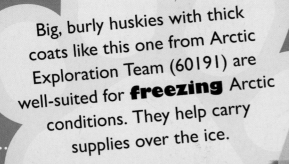

Big, burly huskies with thick coats like this one from Arctic Exploration Team (60191) are well-suited for **freezing** Arctic conditions. They help carry supplies over the ice.

Specially trained dogs help people navigate the world, like the **guide dog** in Town Center (60292). Medically trained dogs also support people who have seizures, diabetes, allergies, and mental health difficulties. Some dogs can even **sniff out diseases!**

BUILDING CHALLENGE!

Try your hand at filmmaking with a stop-motion animation about a heroic dog. A brick-built dog gives lots of options for movement and expressions.

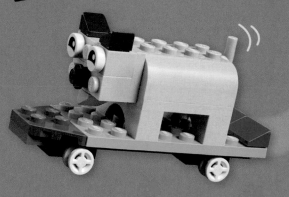

This pug from Bricks on a Roll (10715) loves to **skateboard**. The **fastest** skateboarding dog on record is Jumpy from the US, who whizzed 328 ft (100 m) in **19.65** seconds in 2013.

As well as different breeds of dogs, there are also LEGO **balloon dogs**, minifigures whose jobs revolve around dogs like **Dog Sitter** from the Collectible LEGO Minifigure Series—and even cheery **Hotdog Guy!**

The world's tallest dog was a **Great Dane** called Zeus from Michigan. Towering a whopping 3ft 7in (111.8 cm) above the ground, he was **11 times taller than Milly**—a **Chihuahua** from Puerto Rico and the shortest dog on record.

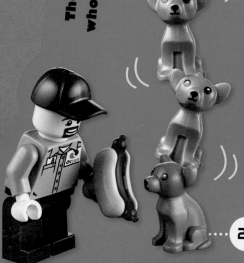

Are you a wiener dog?

In Chinese mythology dragons symbolize **strength** and **power**, and Chinese New Year parades include dragon dances for **good luck**. Several LEGO sets celebrate the festival, including Dragon Dance (80102). The handle can be wound to make the dragon wiggle!

Do LEGO dragons exist?

Yes! Dragons appear across many LEGO themes along with a host of other **magical** and **curious** creatures. Welcome to a **fantastical world** where, with **imagination** and **LEGO bricks**, anything is possible.

Dragons swoop into sets with castles, knights, and Vikings, themes such as LEGO Creator, LEGO® Elves, and LEGO® Wizarding World™. But the **winner** for the most dragons is LEGO® NINJAGO® with **more than 35** of the fiery fiends and friends, including Jungle Dragon (set 71746).

I like to play my flute on the hoof.

Mythological creatures were often based on the human body. This means they make great **minifigures**—like this **faun**.

Fire Dragon (31102)—
LEGO Creator 3-in-1

Fire Dragon Attack (71753)
—LEGO NINJAGO

NEST OF DRAGONS

Aira and Song of the Wind Dragon
(41193)—LEGO Elves

Water Dragon (71754)
—LEGO NINJAGO

A horse with a horn is a **unicorn**. A horse with wings is a **Pegasus**. And a horse with both is an **alicorn**. This one has minifigure wings clipped to its back and a soft, rubbery horn element with a spiral pattern.

What do you get if you cross a horse with a person? A centaur! They come from Greek mythology, and the first one was born from a cloud. Any minifigure torso could fit onto these four horse legs.

Ever since sightings were reported of a mysterious **sea monster** in **Loch Ness**, people have flocked to the Scottish lake in the hope of spotting "**Nessie**." Curved arch pieces make very solid serpentlike coils for this LEGO sea creature, which definitely exists.

BUILDING CHALLENGE!

What wild and wonderful creatures can you make? There are lots of special LEGO pieces, but see what you can make with ordinary pieces—like using a banana piece as a dragon claw.

BUILDING CHALLENGE!

Build something, however big or small. Then see if you can transform it into something else with the same pieces. No sneaking extra ones in!

A jumper plate in the crocodile's mouth can hold the little red **Egyptian plover**. It cleans the crocodile's **teeth**.

LEGO Creator 3-in-1 Crocodile (31121) can be built in three ways to make a crocodile, a snake, or a frog.

Jagged scale pieces on the crocodile become **webbed feet** and smooth body parts on the frog, whose tongue **slides** in and out so it can grab a passing **fly**.

Snakes have a single, long **backbone** of vertebrae. These pieces join together making snakes very **flexible**—just like these brick-built sections that are connected with ball joints.

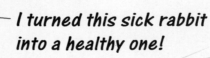

— *I turned this sick rabbit into a healthy one!*

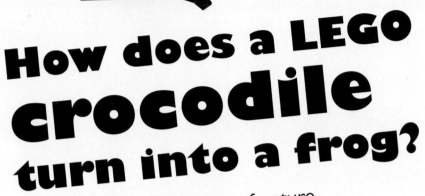

This cool chameleon can change color!

It's used for the **transformation** of a tadpole into a frog—or a caterpillar into a chrysalis and then into a butterfly.

How does a LEGO crocodile turn into a frog?

The **building blocks** of nature **rearrange** themselves as animals are born, grow, and change, sometimes completely altering their appearance. But with LEGO bricks, one **animal** can turn into a totally different one, and LEGO Creator 3-in-1 sets are designed to do just that.

3-in-1 LEGO Creator set **Cute Pug** (30542) can be rebuilt into a **turkey** or a **koala**.

Wild Lion (31112) transforms into a long-legged, long-necked **ostrich** and a muscly, tusked **warthog**.

Lions have **powerful,** bodies for **hunting** and **fighting** off rivals, so they eat a **lot.** They need 15 lb (7 kg) of meat every day —that's the weight of more than **3,000** 2x4 LEGO bricks.

A **tuft** on the end of the warthog's tail is a piece of the lion's mane, and **hooves** are recycled from feathers and fur.

The warthog's tusks make fine **plumage** for the ostrich. The lion's teeth pieces form delicate **feathering** at the end of the wings.

Which LEGO animal lives in the mountains and likes honey?

There are **eight species** of bear on Earth, including American **black** bears, **brown** bears, sloth bears, sun bears, **polar** bears, and **giant pandas**.

Beware the **bears**! The crooks are hiding from the mountain police in Mountain Arrest (60173), but they've strayed into bear territory —and near a beehive. This bear is one of three articulated LEGO bears, seven molded bears, and nine LEGO® DUPLO® bears.

White bricks are best for building **polar bears**, but actually the bears have **black** skin. It's their translucent **fur** that reflects light and makes them look white.

Pandas munch for up to **16 hours** a day, mostly on bamboo. They grip it with a long wrist bone, which they use like a thumb.

American brown bears **communicate** with each other by **scratching** trees.

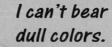

I can't bear dull colors.

There have been **14** colors of LEGO teddy bears since 2012.

This bear is built with black bricks, but not all **black bears** are black. They can also be **blue-gray, brown**, and even **white**.

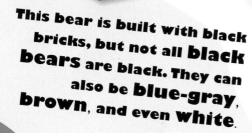

BUILDING CHALLENGE!

What makes a bear? Round ears? Black nose? Sharp claws? How few bricks can you use to build something people can recognize as a bear?

LEGO bears even come in **blue**! Mama and baby bear, Blubeary and Lil' Blu, live in the Crystal Cave in Elvendale, home of the LEGO® Elves theme.

This **grizzly bear's** head is built sideways and joins to the body with two jumper plates. Grizzlies are a sub-species of the American brown bear.

Holes in a 1x2 LEGO Technic brick make two glowing eyes. Real bat eyes also shine in the dark thanks to a special reflective coating in their eye that helps them see for hunting at night.

BUILDING CHALLENGE!

Put on a puppet show with your own LEGO builds and an ordinary flashlight. Give your models plenty of holes to add detail to the silhouettes.

How do you turn a LEGO bat into a shadow puppet?

With a red LEGO light element and a brick-built shadow caster, a simple build like this bat transforms into a striking shadow puppet. Bricks and Lights (11009) includes two sets of shadow casters for shining a light on any LEGO puppet.

These shadows are fangtastic!

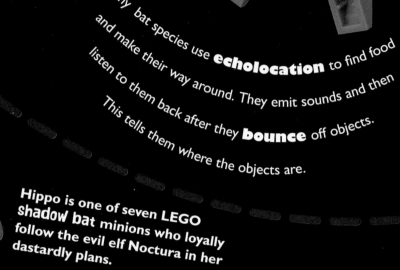

All but a few species of bat sleep **upside down.** Use LEGO clips or elements with rings or holes so you can hang your bat from its **bedtime** perch.

Many bat species use **echolocation** to find food and make their way around. They emit sounds and then listen to them back after they **bounce** off objects. This tells them where the objects are.

We put the bat into battle!

Hippo is one of seven LEGO **shadow bat** minions who loyally follow the evil elf Noctura in her dastardly plans.

The LEGO Elves villain Noctura strikes in the Elvenstar Tree Bat Attack (41196.) The evil elf **shapeshifts** into a **large bat** to wreak havoc on the Elves.

BANG!

Bat droppings are **explosive!** They contain the chemical **potassium nitrate** (saltpeter.) It can be extracted and then used for making **gunpowder.**

How does a LEGO elephant hug?

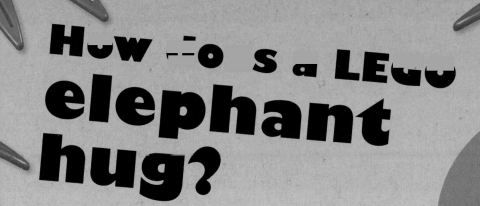

The world's **largest land mammals** are sensitive souls. In times of stress, **elephants** console each other with their **trunks**, even putting them in a distressed elephant's mouth. That's how to **hug the elephant way**! Elephant calves—and sometimes adults—also suck their own trunks for comfort, just like a child sucks their thumb.

BUILDING CHALLENGE!

They say elephants never forget. Build matching pairs of mini LEGO cards then play brain-teasing games to test your memory.

An elephant creates 44 lb (20 kg) of **dung** every day—that's the weight of a **6-year-old child**!

A **newborn elephant** can weigh up to 265 lb (120 kg) —that's the weight of **3,428 minifigures.**

Mice to meet you!

You don't need **trunk** and **tusk** pieces to build LEGO elephants. These models are very different, but they all look like **elephants!**

Separate molds for this LEGO elephant's head and trunk mean they **swivel**. An elephant's trunk can **lift** a staggering 700 lb (317 kg.) That's more than **five average adults**.

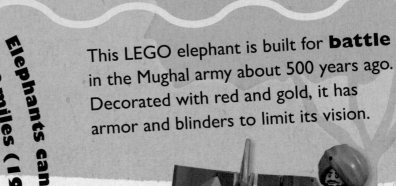

Elephant **tusks** can grow 6 ¾ in (17 cm) a year.

Elephants can **smell water** 12 miles (19 km) away!

This LEGO elephant is built for **battle** in the Mughal army about 500 years ago. Decorated with red and gold, it has armor and blinders to limit its vision.

Elephants' dexterous trunks have about **40,000** muscles. In comparison, a whole person has **less** than **700.**

Vehicles and Transportation

What's the largest LEGO® vehicle?

The LEGO® *Star Wars*™ UCS Millennium Falcon (75192) is the **largest** vehicle, with **7,541 pieces**. At more than 8 in (21 cm) high, 33 in (84 cm) long and 22 in (56 cm) wide it's one of the largest and most detailed LEGO sets ever created and takes about **24 hours** to build.

It's not just the Rebels who command **big** vehicles in LEGO *Star Wars*—the second-largest vehicle is the Imperial Star Destroyer (75252). It might "only" have 4,784 pieces but it's more than 8 in (20 cm) longer than the Millennium Falcon.

Go big! Build a massive LEGO
vehicle. Will it be a land
vehicle with lots of wheels?
Maybe it will be a space
vehicle? What shape
will it be?

OK, but what about the **smallest**
LEGO® vehicle? This open-top Police
Car (30366) is one of the **smallest**
sets with just 37 pieces. It's ideal
for solo police assignments,
as long as it doesn't rain.

*Could you
build a
life-size
LEGO car?*

*Yes, and you can drive it, too!
The LEGO® Technic Bugatti Chiron
is a full-scale working car, made up
of more than 1 million pieces.*

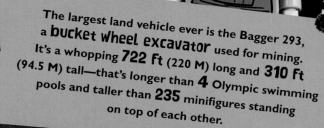

The largest land vehicle ever is the Bagger 293,
a **bucket wheel excavator** used for mining.
It's a whopping **722 ft** (220 M) long and **310 ft**
(94.5 M) tall—that's longer than **4** Olympic swimming
pools and taller than **235** minifigures standing
on top of each other.

The LEGO Bucket Wheel Excavator
(42055) is one of the largest LEGO
Technic sets with 3,929 pieces.

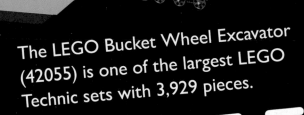

The **longest** vehicles in the
world are **trains**. The longest
train ever was in Australia and
it was more than 4.5 miles
(7.3 km) long. Eight powerful
locomotives pushed 682 cars
filled with iron ore.

It would take this LEGO train (60197)
more than **3 hours** to travel around the
world's longest toy train track. It was built
by an adult LEGO fan (with the help of 80
friends) and uses **93,000 bricks**!

This **enormous** ship is the LEGO® Monkie Kid™ Team Secret HQ (80013). It's got a living area and workshop, but it's also got some useful features for a sea battle. The **crane** can grab enemy boats—if the stud-shooting **water jets** don't put them off first.

A clever captain is as important as a boat in a sea battle. However, the first LEGO boats were made without minifigures. Police Boat (709) in 1978 was the first set to have a minifigure.

There are more than 60 boats in the **LEGO® City** theme alone. Some aren't so good for a sea battle, but have important jobs to do. Container ships like this one carry heavy cargo across the ocean.

The longest container ships measure about **1,312 ft (400 m)**, that's nearly as long as **4 soccer pitches.**

The **fastest speedboat** ever reached speeds of more than 317 mph (510 km/h.)

This LEGO boat is built for **speed** not battle. It has a sleek shape, a bit like a **whale**, and smooth side plates underneath so it can **glide** over surfaces.

It shore is windy today!

Which LEGO boats are good for an epic sea battle?

From classic pirate ships to high-tech submarines, there's a LEGO boat for every **adventure**. However, an epic sea battle calls for something **fast, multi-functional**, and a little bit **fancy**. These LEGO® NINJAGO® catamarans (71748) each have two hulls, which give them great balance, even in shallow water.

BUILDING CHALLENGE!

Look at the shapes of the boats on these pages and build your own ocean vehicle. Is yours built for speed, battle, or to carry heavy cargo?

This **battle** catamaran has 2 spring-loaded shooters and 2 stud shooters. It can also split into **3 separate boats**.

The ninjas' own catamaran can fold up for **speed** mode or fold back out for **attack** mode.

39

Hey, no one told me we were supposed to dress up!

What's the spookiest LEGO tractor?

Without a doubt, the **spookiest** LEGO tractor is in Halloween Hayride (40423). Farms aren't generally spooky (busy, noisy, possibly a bit **smelly**, but not spooky!), but this set is a pumpkin farm with a twist. The costumed minifigures are getting ready for the most **spook-tacular day** of the year—Halloween.

BUILDING CHALLENGE!

Can you build a sturdy tractor? Will it have 4 wheels, or more? What jobs will your tractor do and what extra features does it need?

This vintage-style tractor has a detachable trailer, which is big enough for a minifigure, some hay, and a pumpkin. All aboard for a Halloween hayride!

Tractors have a distinctive design, with large rear **wheels** and smaller front wheels. If you want to build your own, you don't always need a lot of pieces. This simple tractor is built from fewer than **20** LEGO pieces.

HOW FAST CAN A TRACTOR GO?

Most tractors travel at a **steady** speed of around **25 mph** (40 km/h.)

The fastest tractor ever reached speeds of more than **125 mph** (200 km/h.) It had a special engine and a lighter cab, but probably would not have been very good at farm work!

The large rear wheels on this tractor (60287) are ideal for keeping it steady on muddy or **bumpy** ground. It also has a **Loader** bucket and movable **boom**, which are useful for lifting and carrying objects around the farm.

CAN YOU MAKE A LIFE-SIZE LEGO TRACTOR?

Yes! "**Tractobrick**" is a full-scale model built in 2016 using nearly **800,000 LEGO bricks**. It weighs more than a rhino!

WHAT'S THE BIGGEST TRACTOR EVER?

"**Big Bud**" is the biggest tractor ever. This 8-tire machine was built in the US in 1978 and is still working today. It weighs about the same as **18.5 million** 2x4 LEGO bricks.

One of the **biggest** LEGO tractors, the Forest Tractor (60181) doesn't work on a farm. Its long arm with a **huge claw** is designed to pick up massive logs.

How does a LEGO crook make the perfect getaway?

LEGO crooks are not usually the smartest minifigures, but they do have some clever getaway vehicles. In Elite Police Driller Chase (60273), the **crafty** crook uses a mine driller to rob a bank and then **escape underground**. It might not be very subtle, but it's effective!

This LEGO crook attaches a hook to his ATV to bust his friend out of the Mobile Command Center's jail cell (60139). The ATV's **big wheels** mean that these two can make an **off-road** escape.

This **LEGO® Technic Getaway Truck (42090)** is perfect for a **speedy** getaway! With a pull-back motor and huge **chunky** tires, it's ideal for high-speed action!

This truck would be no match for the fastest-ever police car, a Bugatti Veyron in Dubai with a top speed of 253 mph (407 km/h!)

Leaf me alone. The police are stumped!

Heading out to sea can be a great **escape plan**. This speedboat's **streamlined** shape and powerful motor at the stern (back) are perfect for a quick ocean getaway.

This quick-thinking crook has made a **handy raft** with some barrels and wood. It could be a useful getaway vehicle, if the crook remembers to build a **paddle**, too...

The LEGO City police will never look under the water! This crook is making the **perfect** escape in this **minisub**. Or is he? Attaching a **heavy safe** to the back might give him a sinking feeling.

BUILDING CHALLENGE!

Build the perfect getaway vehicle. Will you go for a sleek, speedy shape, or opt for disguise and some handy gadgets?

Some crooks really go the **extra mile** to escape. This sleek **spaceship** will take the crook far away from Earth and the LEGO City Police. But what's she planning to do with those stolen **jewels** in space?

What's the coolest way to get around a LEGO town?

One of the **fastest** cars ever is the SSC Tuatara, which can reach a speed of **282.9 mph** (455.3 km/h.)

This sports car combines **speed** and **style**. It doesn't have a roof, though, so it's not such a fun way to get around on a **rainy day**.

This minifigure thinks it's **cool** to drive an **EV** (Electric Vehicle). EVs run on **batteries**, not fuel. The Town Center set features an EV **charging station** to keep the EV topped up.

With only **three wheels**, this cargo bike is definitely not the fastest vehicle. It's still a **fun** way to get around—unless the "cargo" keeps on wanting to stop for snacks!

EVs are basically **batteries on wheels**, so they can be used to **power** outdoor lights, or even a house.

With more than **700** vehicles in LEGO City, there are plenty of awesome transportation options to suit everyone. From Mayor Fleck's showy stretch limousine (60271) to a speedy skateboard, there are many ways to travel in style.

JM60271

Speed is vital for fighting fires, so this firefighter uses a motorcycle to get around the Town Center (60292.) She can **zoom** in and out of traffic to be first on the scene. A **water tank** on the back also helps her put out small fires.

FIRE-02

Everyone knows that skateboards are the coolest way to get around!

BUILDING CHALLENGE!

What do you think makes a vehicle cool? Is it speed, style, or function? Imagine it, and then build it! That's cool.

Handyman Harl Hubbs can't decide on his coolest vehicle. His **rocket-powered** motorcycle is **super fast** but super noisy. His custom-built cleaning car has space for all his equipment but it only has 3 wheels and is **super slow**.

Which LEGO plan performs incredible loops?

A "loop the loop" is when a plane flies upside down to perform a 360° loop.

propeller

LEGO® Hidden Side El Fuego's Stunt Plane (70429) is not just a buildable **propeller plane**, it can also be connected to an **app** for an awesome ride in a digital world, too.

The **first** LEGO plane landed in stores more than **60** years ago. Since then, hundreds of **fantastic flying LEGO machines** have been created, from hard-working cargo planes to life-saving fire planes. But only very special planes can perform gravity-defying **"loop the loops,"** like this stunt plane.

I'm so dizzy. I must be loopy to do this!

Stunt planes like this one (60323) are small and light but have powerful engines. They can perform lots of **acrobatic** tricks, including loops, dives, turns, and spins.

BUILDING CHALLENGE!

It's time to take to the sky. Will you build a plane that's light enough for stunts or big enough to carry passengers or cargo? Maybe your plane has an important job to do.

The minifigure pilot of this plane cares about **speed**, not acrobatics. This racing plane has cool hinged wings and adjustable tail elevators to make it **super fast**.

This pilot tried a loop the loop in their **seed-planting plane** once, but ended up with a mouthful of seeds. Next time, maybe they should try it when they've finished planting!

The pilot of the **Fire plane** needs all the skill and bravery of the stunt pilot, but her job is to put out fires, not put on a show. Fire planes are filled with **water** to douse **forest fires** or other large-scale blazes.

Can a passenger plane do a loop the loop?

It shouldn't try! For a loop the loop, a plane must be traveling at high speed and able to withstand a strong gravitational force (G force). A commercial plane is **too big, heavy, and slow**—it might break apart.

The first LEGO planes didn't have space for a **pilot** but this huge plane (60262) has room for a pilot, 8 passengers, and even a car!

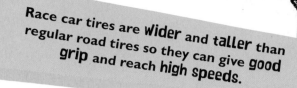
Race car tires are **wider** and **taller** than regular road tires so they can give **good grip** and reach high speeds.

When the first LEGO **wheels** rolled off the production line in 1962, they brought a new dimension to brick play—**movement**. Since then there have been wheels of **all sizes**, to suit all types of vehicles.

Who is one of the biggest tire manufacturers in the world?

The **LEGO Group** makes about **70%** more tires than the next-biggest tire manufacturer, producing more than **700 million** tires per year. Although LEGO tires wouldn't be of any use on a regular car, they're actually very similar to standard tires—even down to the **rubber** they're made from.

Today, there are more than **300** LEGO wheel and tire variants. The **smallest wheels** are on skateboards and measure just ⅓ **in** (8mm) in diameter.

BUILDING CHALLENGE!

Count your LEGO wheels. Some Australian road trains (long trucks) have over 100 wheels. Build your own mega-multi-wheel vehicle. Will it be long like a train, or tall like a Thricycle?

Superbikes, like this one, are also designed for **speed**. The **wide tires** and powerful engine combine to produce awesome **power** and **grip**.

LEGO City Cargo Plane (7734) has the most tires of any individual road vehicle with 14.

I might need to rethink my getaway car!

The first car tires were **white**, because that's the natural color of rubber. They became **black** when carbon (and later silica) was added. Only **one LEGO set** has ever had white tires: LEGO® Spongebob Squarepants™ Bikini Bottom Express (3830).

CAN YOU BUILD A THREE-WHEELED BIKE?

Yes! Check out this "Thricycle" from Master Builder Emmet. It might be unconventional and a little tricky to balance on, but it looks AWESOME!

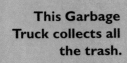

This Garbage Truck collects all the trash.

LEGO trucks don't just serve up food. Check out these other useful LEGO vehicles.

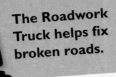

Garbage Truck
(60220)

Fire Ladder Truck
(60280)

This Fire Ladder Truck races to put out fires.

The Roadwork Truck helps fix broken roads.

Roadwork Truck
(60284)

The **world record** for the **fastest** electric **ice cream truck** is **80.03 mph** (128.8 km/h.) Now that would make a great getaway vehicle!

Don't be fooled by this **cute truck** (80009)! With its refrigerator and **piggy shooter** on top, it's fully equipped to do **battle** with food-stealing baddies.

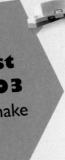

Ice Cream

Real Ice Cream

JH 60314

Well, I can make a speedy triple scoop!

This **ice cream truck** (60314) looks pretty **tasty**, but it's all part of a **clever plot**. The bank robbers spray the LEGO police with ice cream to **distract** them as they rob the bank! What a **delicious** plan.

What's the tastiest-looking LEGO truck?

With a **giant burger** proudly decorating its roof, this is surely the **tastiest**-looking LEGO truck (31104). Plus, its **huge monster wheels** mean that it can head **off road** to serve up tasty burgers pretty much anywhere. Hungry minifigures just have to make sure they "ketchup" with it!

BUILDING CHALLENGE!

Get trucking! Be bold—maybe you can build the world's first underwater ice cream truck or a jet-powered garbage truck.

Which LEGO submarine can also drive on land?

Most submarines only travel **underwater** but with a LEGO vehicle, anything is possible. Ninjas Cole and Jay can travel to **mysterious** underwater worlds or continue their adventure on **dry land** in their versatile **Ninja Sub Speeder** (71752), which has both submarine and car modes.

Some submarines can stay **underwater** for **months** at a time.

Most jellyfish are **harmless** to humans, but the **sea wasp jellyfish** is the world's most **venomous** jellyfish.

Jay battles the villainous **Hammer Head** in his **Flying Jelly Sub** (70610). The design of the villain's submarine is inspired by ocean **jellyfish** who use their tentacles to **sting** predators or **stun** their **prey**.

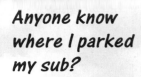

Anyone know where I parked my sub?

BUILDING CHALLENGE!

Build an epic underwater vehicle. How big will it be? Will you use it to hunt for treasure or to study ocean life? Can your sub also travel on land? Maybe it can even fly!

Scientist and inventor J.B. has built her own awesome submarine (70433) to hunt underwater **ghosts**. It has a clear windshield and **powerful headlights** for maximum visibility, plus two **grabbers** at the front, ready to catch a **specter**.

Sometimes a **small** submarine is best for a **secret** underwater treasure hunt. This **mini sub** (60263) only has space for one minifigure but its long "arms" are ideal for grabbing **sunken treasure**.

Sometimes a submarine doesn't even need a **pilot**. This **robot sub** (31045) can be **operated remotely** to collect underwater data.

The Ocean Exploration Submarine (60264) is well equipped to investigate **ocean life**. It has **four** powerful **propellers** so it can travel down to the **sea bed**, and bright searchlights to guide its way.

The first **steam locomotive** was built by British engineer Richard Trevithick in **1804**.

The **first trains** were powered by **steam** produced by burning coal.

LEGO trains have been around for **90** years, long before the LEGO brick was invented. The first trains launched in the **1930s** and were **wooden** with no carriages.

Underground trains are a great way to avoid crowds and **traffic** in the city. They carry passengers through **tunnels** deep under the city.

Nowadays, most trains run on **electricity**. The first high-speed railroad was built in **Japan** in the 1960s. High-speed trains have a streamlined shape, like this one.

BUILDING CHALLENGE!

Design your own LEGO train. Start with the locomotive: will it be electric or steam? Will you add carriages or freight cars? Perhaps your train could travel on rails and the road, or maybe it will be super long!

Which **LEGO** train has the most valuable cargo?

The **12 gold bars** carried by the LEGO City Cargo Train (60198) are the **most valuable** cargo. Featuring an impressive **1,226** pieces, including a driver's cabin, **three wagons**, plus an armoured truck and a forklift—this amazing train set is bursting with play potential.

More than **25 passenger trains** have made the journey into LEGO sets. LEGO City Passenger Train (60197) features a **motorized** engine with 10-speed Bluetooth remote control plus a café and passenger cars with removable roofs, seats, and tables.

Phew! It's hot and smelly work driving a steam train!

Train carriages or cars are **pushed** or **pulled** by an engine called a **locomotive**. They are powered by steam or electricity.

How does LEGO® City keep its streets clean and tidy?

Some **heroes** wear capes, but in LEGO City there's a super team of **everyday** heroes who work hard to keep the streets **clean and tidy**. This minifigure drives the **Street Sweeper** (60249) and sweeps dirt and garbage away with two types of rotating brushes.

big rotating brushes

smaller rotating brushes

A lot of **waste** can be **recycled** into something else. The **crane** lifts the huge recycling units onto the back of the **recycling truck** and takes them away to be sorted and the garbage made into something new.

» **Cardboard** can be recycled at least **7** times.
» **Glass** can be recycled **endlessly**.
» **Recycled plastic** can also be used to make playground equipment, clothes, and furniture.

JM60292

BUILDING CHALLENGE!

Can you design a super cleaning vehicle? Maybe it will have brushes for sweeping, a hose for cleaning, or even a special grabbing arm to pick up garbage.

The average person creates more than **4 ½ lb** (2 kg) of trash every day. This vehicle empties the dumpsters regularly so they don't get too full.

I'd better pick this up before someone slips on it!

It's the job of some minifigures to keep everything **working** in LEGO City. This truck has a special **crane arm** to lift the driver up to **fix** the streetlight.

Heavy **snow** is no problem in LEGO City. The **Snow Groomer** (60222) has a large **plow** on the front to push the snow away and clear the roads.

How does a LEGO helicopter pick up a stolen safe?

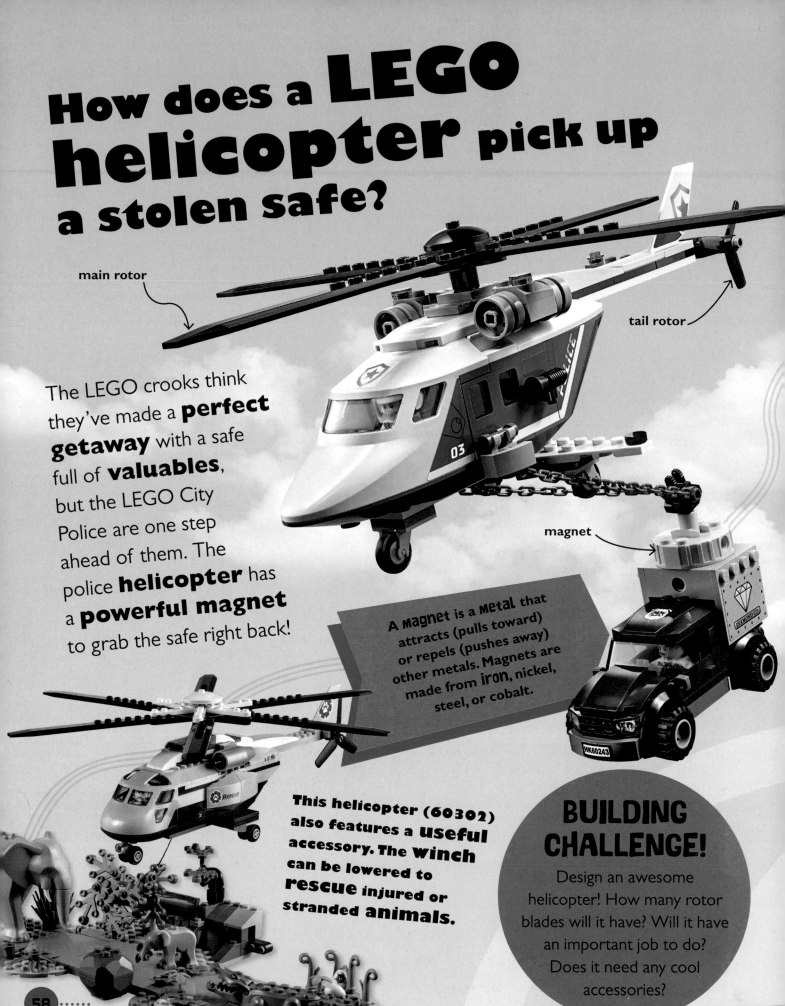

main rotor

tail rotor

magnet

The LEGO crooks think they've made a **perfect getaway** with a safe full of **valuables**, but the LEGO City Police are one step ahead of them. The police **helicopter** has a **powerful magnet** to grab the safe right back!

A **magnet** is a metal that attracts (pulls toward) or repels (pushes away) other metals. Magnets are made from iron, nickel, steel, or cobalt.

This helicopter (60302) also features a **useful** accessory. The **winch** can be lowered to **rescue** injured or stranded **animals**.

BUILDING CHALLENGE!

Design an awesome helicopter! How many rotor blades will it have? Will it have an important job to do? Does it need any cool accessories?

HELICOPTER FACTS

Helicopters are versatile vehicles. They can:

» **Take off** and land **vertically**
» **Hover** in one spot in the air
» Fly **backward** or sideways
» Lift **heavy** objects
» Fly to **hard-to-reach** places

water cannons

This **fire helicopter** (60281) can reach a blaze fast and then use its **water cannons** to put the fire out quickly.

This **ambulance helicopter** (60179) can collect patients that road vehicles can't reach. Its **"landing skids"** hold it steady in small or uneven landing spots.

landing skids

Thanks for rescuing me!

Drones are similar to helicopters, but they are usually controlled remotely. Monkie Kid's **dronecopter** (80023) combines the best features of both machines—four rotor blades like a drone, but with space for a pilot!

This simple helicopter build has **one rotor** that **rotates** on a **pin**. The landing skids are made of **3x1** pieces.

How **does** a LEGO **buggy** put out a forest **fire?**

Buggies are some of the toughest LEGO vehicles, despite also being some of the smallest. This little but **sturdy fire buggy** (60247) is more than a match for a forest fire. It's fitted with a cool **water cannon**, ready to **blast** the **flames** before they can spread.

water cannon

Buggies, ATVs (**All Terrain Vehicles**), and quad bikes are all similar types of small vehicle designed to be driven "off-road."

Baja vehicles are named after a famously tough off-road race in Mexico, the Baja 1000.

Green Ninja Lloyd's buggy is built for **speed**. It has a **sleek** racing car shape, plus **chunky tires** for grip and balance. The **gold swords** look cool and may come in handy if peace in NINJAGO is threatened.

gold katana

This Baja **race buggy** (60288) is not just built for speed, it's also able to handle the toughest off-road conditions. The buggy is **steerable** and comes with a choice of two minifigure drivers.

This Off-Road Buggy (42124) is super fun to build, ideal for performing cool **tricks and stunts**, and it can also be **controlled remotely** via a smartphone app.

Buggies bug me. They can't even fly!

This **quad bike** (41442) is perfect for exploring **nature**. It's also fully equipped to **help animals** in need, with a handy **winch** to remove fallen trees, a **feeding bottle**, and a compartment big enough to transport an injured animal to the **vet** clinic.

feeding bottle

Dune Buggy (31087) has **chunky tires** to help it balance on shifting **sand dunes**. It can also be rebuilt into a plane or quad bike.

BUILDING CHALLENGE!

Find four chunky tires and build the coolest buggy ever. Will it perform stunts, win races, drive to the rescue, or be equipped to explore outer space?

The coolest LEGO buggy of all might just be this **space buggy** (951911). Space buggies have to be **robust** enough to cope with bumpy terrain, such as on the moon, but **small and light** enough to fit inside a space shuttle.

CHAPTER 3

Technology
and
Inventions

Which LEGO® plants are made from plants?

All **180** botanical elements in the LEGO® Ideas Tree House (21318) are made from sustainably sourced **sugarcane**. That includes the leaves on the tree and the plants around it. It's part of the LEGO **"Plants from Plants"** campaign, where sugarcane is turned into a special **plastic** that is kinder to the environment.

"Sustainably sourced" means made from something that is unlikely to ever run out.

Why does a deciduous tree **shed** its leaves in the fall? Because it has used up all the nutrients in them. Fall leaves turn all kinds of **warm colors** before they fall. These yellow and brown LEGO leaves are perfect for your fall builds.

Roses, daisies, or asters? Take your pick in the LEGO® Creator Flower Bouquet (10280). With its **posable** petals and **adjustable** stems, it includes lots of new pieces made from plant-based plastic.

Sugarcane can only be cultivated in hot parts of the world.

The stalks grow up to **26 ft (8m)** tall and can be white, yellow, green, purple, or red.

Bonsai is the ancient art of growing miniature trees. This LEGO tree is **7 in (18 cm)** tall—about the size of a real bonsai tree. Its pink foliage is made from plant-based plastic and looks just like **cherry blossom.**

Hey, what are we celebrating?

BUILDING CHALLENGE!

Plantus Maximus is a special sustainable LEGO superhero! Why not build a hero of your own using LEGO bricks combined with flower and leaf elements?

Building a sustainable future!

What's the most thrilling LEGO roller coaster?

If it's ups, downs, twists, and turns you want, the LEGO Creator Expert Roller Coaster (10261) can't be beaten. This mammoth coaster has a **chain lift** to haul the cars to the dizzying height of **21 in (53 cm)**. It's all downhill from there, so hold on to your minifigure hat and smile for the **camera**!

BUILDING CHALLENGE!

A roller coaster car doesn't have to look like a car. Can you build one that looks like a dragon or a monster? Don't forget to add wheels!

In the US, **August 16th** is National Roller Coaster Day.

Most roller coasters won't accept young riders below a **certain height.** This little minifigure doesn't quite measure up!

The **fastest** roller coaster in the world is Formula Rossa in United Arab Emirates. This hair-raising ride travels at up to 149.1 mph (240 kph) and can accelerate from 0 to 62 mph (100 kph) in just **two seconds!**

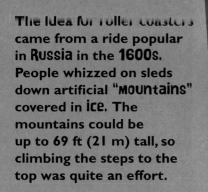

The idea for roller coasters came from a ride popular in Russia in the 1600s. People whizzed on sleds down artificial "mountains" covered in ice. The mountains could be up to 69 ft (21 m) tall, so climbing the steps to the top was quite an effort.

Ahoy there! The roller coaster in LEGO® Friends Heartlake City Amusement Pier (41375) has a **pirate ship** theme. Even the car is shaped like a little **boat**.

Try building a simple LEGO roller coaster. All you need are curved arch bricks and tiles to make an up-and-down track.

In LEGO® Hidden Side Haunted Fairground (70432), passengers pass through a posse of **ghosts**. Scream if you want to go faster. Or just scream…

So how did our **minifigures** enjoy the ride?

Best ride ever!

It was brilliant!

I shouldn't have had that third ice cream…

Which LEGO mech mines for space crystals?

BUILDING CHALLENGE!
Build a simple mech, then cover it with different LEGO parts to look like high-tech details. Grilles, antennas, tubes, and wrenches are good.

Most mechs are built for battle, but not the LEGO Creator Space Mining Mech (31115). Shiny green crystals is all this minifigure mech pilot wants. The mech uses a **buzzsaw** to cut the crystals from the space rock, then stashes them in its **jetpack**. They must be valuable, because this **alien** is after them, too!

Is a mech just a giant **robot**? No. A mech is operated by an onboard **pilot**, whereas a robot has to be **programmed** to do things.

Mechs are **walking** machines, so they have to be stable. Make sure your mech has big **feet**, like this small blue-and-white one.

In 2020 scientists succeeded in building a real-life mech called Prosthesis. It's **15 ft (4.5 m)** tall, has 4 legs, and is powerful enough to **lift a car**. The creators are now working on building much faster mechs. They hope to make **mech-racing** a popular sport one day.

THE LEGO® NINJAGO® NINJA HAVE THE PERFECT MECH FOR ANY BATTLE. TAKE A PEEK INSIDE THEIR HANGAR TO SEE JUST A FEW.

Fire Stone Mech (71720)

Jay's Electro Mech (71740)

Kai's Mech Jet (71707)

Zane's Titan Mech Battle (71738)

Lloyd's Hydro Mech (71750)

Hi, I'm Evil Mech. I'm here to mech trouble.

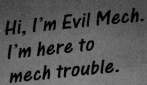

Some mechs are shaped like real or mythical animals. LEGO® Monkie Kid™ Guardian Lion Mech (80021) is inspired by the **lion statues** that stand outside many **Chinese** buildings. Their job is to scare away evil. Monkie Kid's mech does that, too!

What's the weirdest LEGO science lab?

They don't come weirder than **J.B.'s Ghost Lab** (70418) from LEGO Hidden Side. Why? Because it combines science with specters! There's a **de-haunting chamber** in the middle, with a long electrical coil to zap away ghosts that have possessed minifigures. That's not just weird—it's shocking!

Astronauts have grown lettuce in the lab on the **International Space Station.** Some of them thought it tasted a bit weird!

A **DNA** double helix is tiny because it is so tightly coiled. Scientists have calculated that if uncoiled, all the **DNA** in your body would be about twice the diameter of our solar system!

BUILDING CHALLENGE!

Build a lab—then use LEGO pipes and hoses to connect the different bits of equipment. What strange potions might be flowing through them?

Spider Queen watches her assistant, Syntax, build robot spiders in her lab (80022). After **attacking her enemies**, the spiders can be taken apart for storage in the lab. Until next time...

NASA's **Curiosity Rover** trundles over Mars, **sampling dust** in its onboard lab. The LEGO version (21104) is only 6 in (15 cm) long but has many details, including a **camera** on an extendable "selfie stick" at the front.

The **baby robot** in Olivia's Creative Lab (41307) is tiny, but there's a real-life bot that's tinier. RoboBee is a flying robot no bigger than a bug!

Dozens of LEGO scientist minifigures have been released, including the collectible **Monster Scientist** with his dangerous-looking **experiment**.

I'm the smartest!

What a brainy bunch!

An operator changes the drone's **direction** by adjusting the speed of individual rotors. LEGO® Technic pins are a good way of attaching the rotors to drone builds so they can turn freely.

Which LEGO drone can scout out fires?

Fire down below! The drone from LEGO Fire Station (60215) is designed to spot **blazes** before they get out of hand. Four spinning rotors get the drone **airborne** over the city. When it finds a **fire**, its rotating camera sends live images back to the LEGO® City firefighters, who **rush** to the scene with their hoses.

BUILDING CHALLENGE!

Build a variety of drones with different kinds of rotors. You could use propellors, steering wheels, or even make your own from 1x6 plates.

How high do drones fly? In most countries they are not allowed to go higher than 394 ft (120 m), in case they collide with aircraft!

Chasing criminals...

Police Patrol Boat (60277) LEGO City

Exploring space...

Mars Research Shuttle (60226) LEGO City

AMAZING DRONE JOBS

Attempting robberies...

Spying on undersea enemies...

Sky Police Drone Chase (60207) LEGO City

Ninja Sub Speeder (71752) LEGO NINJAGO

I fly my drone strictly for fun. Just call me Drone Boy!

Anywhere at all...

Drone Explorer (31071) LEGO Creator

Tracking wild animals...

Rescue ATV (60300) LEGO City

Scientists have used a drone to collect **whale DNA** for animal research. They did it by flying the drone through the blast of snot from the whale's blowhole. **Yuk!**

In **Australia**, drones help **prevent** shark attacks. If a drone spies a shark close to the shore it plays a message **warning** swimmers to get out of the water. A drone can spot a shark with 90% accuracy—more than **three** times better than a human lookout.

Can you power a LEGO house with renewable energy?

Just one **solar panel** on the roof can power an entire two-story LEGO house. The LEGO Creator Modular Modern Home (31068) has a solar skylight that tilts to gather energy from the sun. What's more, it powers a charging station for an **electric car**, too. Bring on the sun!

BUILDING CHALLENGE!

Build a house with a pitched roof, then cover it with blue tiles to represent solar panels. How many can you fit on your roof?

Wow... there's a lot of wind today.

Burp!

A **boat** named MS Tûranor PlanetSolar circumnavigated the world powered only by sunshine. Its solar panels are a massive 5,382 sq ft (500 sq m), and cover much of its roof.

Today, we use the force from water flowing through **dams** to create electricity. But water power is not new. In medieval times, **water wheels** powered mills for grinding flour.

What's the weather like today—sunny or windy? Olivia doesn't mind! Her car charger runs on both solar and wind power in LEGO Friends Olivia's Electric Car (41443).

Energy from the sun and wind is also known as **clean energy**.

It doesn't pollute the **atmosphere** like burning coal or gas does.

Wind farms are groups of wind turbines. They are often built at sea, where it's really gusty. The largest offshore wind farm is Hornsea One, off the coast of England. It creates enough electricity to power more than a **million** homes.

Cable cars help make **city air** cleaner. They run on electricity from overhead **cables**, not pollution-creating fuel. This LEGO cable car has a pivoting joint halfway along so it can go around bends.

How does a wind **turbine** work? Its **blades** are connected by a shaft to a **generator**. As the wind turns the blades, the generator creates electricity. This LEGO wind turbine has blades that really turn, thanks to a LEGO Technic pin.

When **talking pictures** arrived in the 1930s, going to the movie theater became all the rage. Heartlake City Movie Theater is based on the glamorous **"picture palaces"** of the time. It's dotted with round tiles that look like yellow **neon lights.**

Which LEGO theater lets you screen films?

What's showing at the LEGO Friends Heartlake City Movie Theater (41448)? Any movie you like… maybe even one you made yourself! In this vintage-style theater, your **smartphone** can become the **screen**. Don't forget the LEGO popcorn for VIP guests!

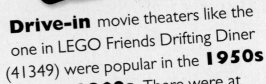

Drive-in movie theaters like the one in LEGO Friends Drifting Diner (41349) were popular in the **1950s and 1960s**. There were at least 4,000 of them in the US. That's more than **11 times** the number of bricks in the Drifting Diner set.

BUILDING CHALLENGE!

Theater seating is tiered so everyone can see the screen. Stack up bricks, plates, and chairs to build rows of seats that increase in height.

My first movie! My first award!

Popcorn was banned in early movie theaters. The management thought it was noisy, messy, and just not very classy.

Which LEGO set plays music?

You don't have to be a maestro to play **sweet music**. All you need is your smartphone, the Powered Up app, and the **LEGO Grand Piano** (21323). The concert-style piano has moving **keys, hammers, and pedals**, just like a real one. Are you ready to tickle the bricks?

A thumb piano—or **mbira**—is nothing like a grand piano. This small African instrument has little metal **"tongues"** that the musician plucks to make sweet, soft sounds.

The **harpsichord** was a popular instrument to play at concerts in the Baroque period. It was a cross between a piano and a guitar—when you pressed the keys, it **plucked** its own strings, making a sharp, clear sound.

I think I just broke another string!

LEGO **guitars** come in a variety of different shapes and sizes—from a pop star's **electric** guitar in Andrea's Musical Duet (41309) to a Mariachi's **classical** guitar. There's even a jazzy **keytar** for minifigures who like '80s music to play!

Mariachi
Series 16 (71013)

Jacob
Tournament of Elements
(71735) LEGO NINJAGO

80s Musician
Series 20 (71027)

Monster Rocker
Series 14 (71010)

Rock Star
Series 12 (71007)

Bedroom (10926)
LEGO DUPLO

BUILDING CHALLENGE!

Build a smashing drum kit for a minifigure. Round bricks topped with round tiles make good drums, and radar dishes on poles are perfect for the cymbals.

The **gramophone** was an early record player invented in **1888**. It sounded crackly and you had to keep winding it up, but at last people could listen to music without waiting for a live performance.

BUILDING CHALLENGE!

Make a LEGO X-ray of a hand by attaching black and white bricks to a tile base, mosaic style. Will your X-ray show a broken finger?

X-rays **pass through** soft things like muscle but are blocked by hard things. That's why **bones** show up white on X-ray pictures.

How does a LEGO doctor examine X-rays?

A stethoscope lets the doctor listen to a patient's **heart** and **lungs**. This LEGO stethoscope has a flexible tube and ear plugs made of round plates.

In LEGO City Hospital (60204) the doctor on the first floor uses a **light brick** to **project** a large image of an X-ray onto the wall. Ah, that's a lovely, clear picture. Now we can see why this patient is feeling sore.

Your **transportation** awaits! A patient gets ready for a ride home after their hospital visit (60330). The **ramp** in the ambulance will make loading the wheelchair a breeze.

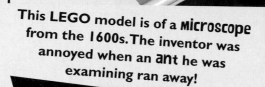

This LEGO model is of a MICROSCOPE from the 1600s. The inventor was annoyed when an ANT he was examining ran away!

Great news from the lab, the samples are clear!

At a hospital, doctors can test **samples** from patients to check for different **illnesses**.

There have been **24** doctor minifigures released in the LEGO City theme alone. This one (952105) is very pleased to treat you!

A minifigure patient in this set (60204) is having a **vision** test. They peer through a machine called a **phoropter** and read letters from a **chart**. The eye doctor adjusts the lenses on the machine until the patient can see clearly. Now they know what glasses to prescribe!

81

Which LEGO typewriter has working keys?

Tap, tap, tap... that's the sound of the LEGO Ideas typewriter. Like a real old-fashioned typewriter, this set (21327) has big, round, **noisy keys** that make **levers** spring up as you press them. A complicated system of LEGO Technic pieces cleverly controls the movement.

Computers replaced typewriters in the 1980s, but their keyboards have the same QWERTY layout.

BUILDING CHALLENGE!

Modern satellites have "wings" that tilt to collect solar energy. Build a satellite using tiles for the wings, and use plates with bars to attach them.

A morning paper makes the commute fly by for minifigures at the LEGO City Bus Station (60154). These copies of The LEGO News are 2x2 tiles with special printing.

NEWSSTAND

THROUGHOUT HISTORY, ALL KINDS OF INVENTIONS HAVE HELPED PEOPLE COMMUNICATE:

Printing press
1845

Telegraph cables
1830s

Telephone
1876

Home computers
1980s

TV
1920s

World Wide Web
1990

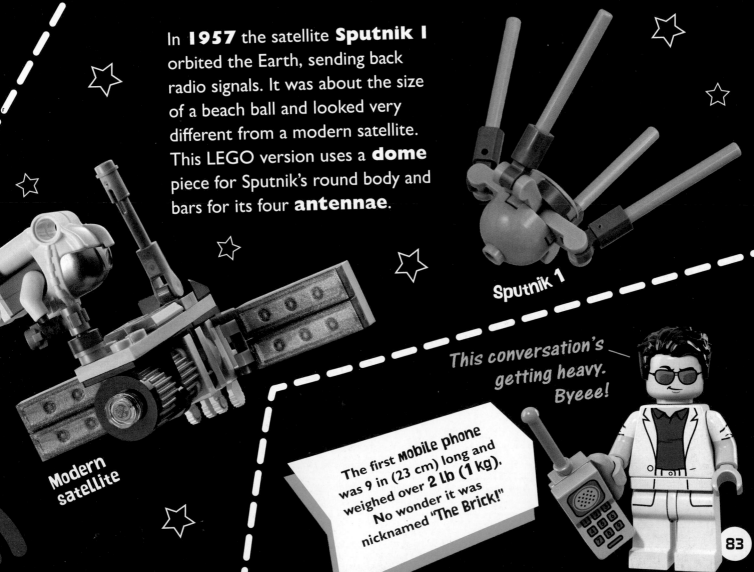

In **1957** the satellite **Sputnik 1** orbited the Earth, sending back radio signals. It was about the size of a beach ball and looked very different from a modern satellite. This LEGO version uses a **dome** piece for Sputnik's round body and bars for its four **antennae**.

Sputnik 1

Modern satellite

This conversation's getting heavy. Byeee!

The first mobile phone was **9 in (23 cm)** long and weighed over **2 lb (1 kg)**. No wonder it was nicknamed 'The Brick!'

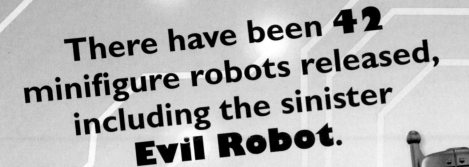

There have been **42** minifigure robots released, including the sinister **Evil Robot.**

Don't worry... I'll reprogram him if he does anything too evil!

Which LEGO robot has the most skills?

LEGO robots can do many things, but one is especially versatile. Roll forward **Vernie** from LEGO® BOOST Creative Toolbox (17101). With the right **coding**, Vernie can talk, dance, shoot a target, play hockey, and even beatbox.

Robots aren't all made of metal. The softest is "Octobot." It's based on a real octopus, with eight legs and a squishy silicon body.

LEGO® MINDSTORMS® Robot inventor (51515) includes five fabulous robots, all remotely controlled via an app.

Charlie (51515)

This little helper is made for robot dancing and drumming, too.

M.V.P. (51515)

If there's lifting and shifting to be done, M.V.P. is your robot.

The first humanlike robot caused a sensation at the New York World's Fair in **1939**.

It was 7 ft (2.1 m) tall, spoke, blew up **balloons**, and had a **robot dog** called Sparko.

Blast (51515)

Blast uses missiles, punches, and a hammer to defend his builder's toys.

Gelo (51515)

Four footed, sure-footed Gelo dodges any obstacles in his path.

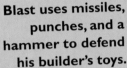

TRICKY (51515)

Tricky is a whiz at soccer, bowling, basketball, and drawing!

BUILDING CHALLENGE!

Think of a job to be done— then build a robot to do it. A robot with extendable arms would be ideal for putting things on high shelves.

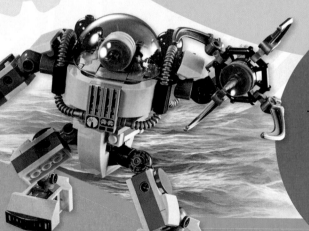

Finding **sunken treasure** is the mission of the LEGO Creator 3-in-1 Underwater Robot (31090). In 2016, a real robot did the same when it recovered a vase from a ship that sank in **1664**.

Tea, anyone? Serving hot drinks is a boring task for this LEGO robot. But boring work is exactly what robots were first built for. In fact the word "robot" means "servitude" in Czech.

Which LEGO set goes off with a bang?

The Story of Nian (80106) is a cracker of a LEGO set. It features a **Chinese** house decked out for Lunar New Year. With buildable **fireworks** on the roof and **firecrackers** at the ready, the residents will scare off that menacing Nian beast in a flash!

Which bright spark put the zipper at the back?

BUILDING CHALLENGE!

Build a batch of colorful LEGO rockets. Use stacked round plates to make striped bodies, then top them with cones and add bars for the sticks.

This minifigure is welcoming in the Year of the Ox with a string of firecrackers made from red bar holders with clips.

BANG

How do fireworks get their dazzling colors?

It's all down to the metal salts they contain. For example, **copper** creates blue sparks and **strontium** red ones.

Fireworks were invented in China about 1,000 years ago. People stuffed **bamboo** stems with **gunpowder**, set them alight, and waited for the bang. This brick-built firework uses a LEGO telescope piece for the fuse.

The fireworks that launch from LEGO® Disney Princess™ Ariel's Royal Celebration Boat (41153) are heart shaped. Well, it is the wedding of Ariel and Prince Eric that's being celebrated!

Shhh… the winner of Andrea's Talent Show (41368) is about to be announced. Watch out for fireworks shooting from the **stage canopy**.

Firework pieces **shoot out** from holders when they are pressed.

The largest ever firework display took place in the Philippines on January 1, 2016. The **hour-long** display included **810,904** fireworks.

CHAPTER 4
Architecture

H—w t— —ll i— ——a LEGO® lighthouse?

The Jeddah Light in Saudi Arabia, which is a whopping **436 ft (133 m)** high!

LEGO® lighthouses come in many different heights, from tiny mini models to a **tottering multi-story** LEGO® NINJAGO® lighthouse measuring over **14 in (36 cm)**. It needs to be tall in order to fit in all the traps the ninja have set for their pirate enemies, from collapsing floors to escape pipes!

BUILDING CHALLENGE!

First build a lighthouse using round bricks—then see if you can build another round one using straight bricks. How many levels can you add?

Lighthouse keeping is a tricky job. I'm a shining example!

Over 6 ½ in (17 cm)

Fire Boat (60109) – LEGO City

LEGO LIGHTHOUSE LINEUP

Over 14 in (36 cm)

Over 11 in (29 cm)

Over 11 in (29 cm)

The Lighthouse Siege (70594)
– LEGO NINJAGO

The Lighthouse of Darkness (70431)
– LEGO Hidden Side

Lighthouse Rescue Centre (41380) – LEGO FRIENDS

Over 9 in (23 cm)

Over 7 in (18 cm)

Over 5 ½ in (14 cm)

Over 3 ½ in (9 cm)

Over 3 ½ in (9 cm)

Lighthouse Point (31051)
– LEGO Creator

**Heartlake Lighthouse (41094) –
LEGO FRIENDS**

**Elite Police
Lighthouse Capture
(60274) – LEGO City**

**Heavy-duty
Rescue Helicopter
(60166) – LEGO City**

**Fire Boat
(10591)
– LEGO DUPLO**

You don't need lots of bricks to build an impressive lighthouse. This **micro-scale model** only uses a few bricks, but it still packs a punch with its **striped tower**, and **tan-colored pieces** that create an island.

The most famous lighthouse ever is probably the **Lighthouse of Alexandria**. It was built in the 3rd century BCE and was one of the Seven Wonders of the Ancient World. It's estimated to have been at least **328 ft (100 m) tall**, before it was ruined by earthquakes.

Which LEGO® Architecture city features giant solar-powered supertrees?

The city of **Singapore** has a forest of **Supertrees**: huge flowerlike structures that incorporate real plants, metal sculpture, and light displays. The LEGO Architecture set includes six of these in mini scale sitting alongside other key landmarks, which makes a recognizable **snapshot** of the famous city.

I'm a Master City Builder!

Marina Bay Sands

One Raffles Place

OCBC Center

Singapore

Supertree Grove

The Fullerton Hotel

SINGAPORE (21057)

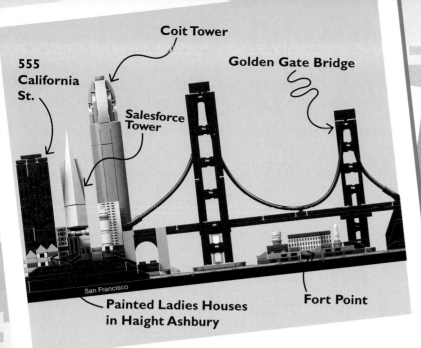

555 California St.

Coit Tower

Golden Gate Bridge

Salesforce Tower

Painted Ladies Houses in Haight Ashbury

Fort Point

San Francisco

SAN FRANCISCO (21043)

National Gallery

London Eye

London

Nelson's Column

Big Ben (Elizabeth Tower)

Tower Bridge

LONDON (21034)

BUILDING CHALLENGE!

Can you build a skyline model of where you live? Think about the scale of the buildings and features.

Tokyo Tower

Mode Gakuen Cocoon Tower

Tokyo Skytree

Pagoda

Mount Fuji

Tokyo Big Sight

Tokyo

Chidorigafuchi Park

TOKYO (21051)

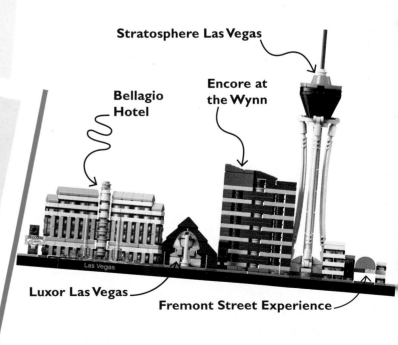

Stratosphere Las Vegas

Bellagio Hotel

Encore at the Wynn

Las Vegas

Luxor Las Vegas

Fremont Street Experience

LAS VEGAS (21047)

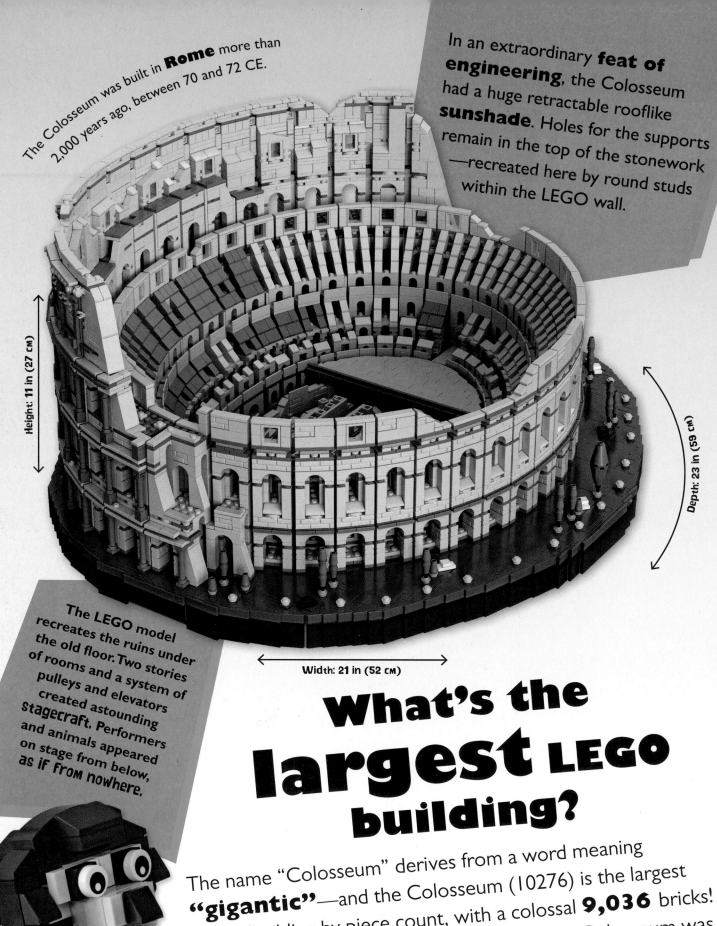

The Colosseum was built in **Rome** more than 2,000 years ago, between 70 and 72 CE.

In an extraordinary **feat of engineering**, the Colosseum had a huge retractable rooflike **sunshade**. Holes for the supports remain in the top of the stonework —recreated here by round studs within the LEGO wall.

Height: 11 in (27 CM)

Depth: 23 in (59 CM)

The **LEGO model** recreates the ruins under the old floor. Two stories of rooms and a system of pulleys and elevators created astounding **stagecraft**. Performers and animals appeared on stage from below, as if from nowhere.

Width: 21 in (52 CM)

What's the largest LEGO building?

The name "Colosseum" derives from a word meaning **"gigantic"**—and the Colosseum (10276) is the largest LEGO building by piece count, with a colossal **9,036** bricks! A symbol of the Ancient Roman Empire, the Colosseum was a huge amphitheater for entertainment such as gladiatorial battles.

The Colosseum has four types of pillar. The LEGO model uses tan **candle** pieces, with a **roller skate** piece for the Ionic column and a **flower** to top the frilly Corinthian design.

DORIC

IONIC

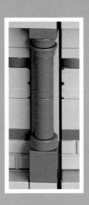
CORINTHIAN

PILASTER

The LEGO model recreates the **Colosseum** today. Two thousand years ago, the outer wall was **solid** all the way around, but it has disappeared over time.

Crowds watched gladiators fight. These warriors trained in special schools and were often injured in battle. Many used swords, but the retiarius gladiators fought with a trident.

For the glory of Rome!

Sometimes gladiators fought **wild animals**, including lions, crocodiles, rhinos, hippos, elephants, and bears.

TOP 5 LEGO BUILDINGS WITH THE MOST BRICKS

1 LEGO The Colosseum (10276) – **9,036** pieces.

2 LEGO® Harry Potter™ Hogwarts Castle (71043) – **6,020** pieces

3 LEGO The Taj Mahal (10189 / 10256) – **5,922 / 5,923** pieces

4 LEGO NINJAGO City Gardens (71741) – **5,685** pieces

Which LEGO castle can take you into space?

The LEGO® NEXO KNIGHTS™ **Knighton Castle** (70357) is out of this world. Its top tower is a **rocket**! Medieval castles have been around for more than a thousand years, inspiring tales of **bravery** and **adventure**.

Battlements, or crenellations, on castle walls protected soldiers, while also letting them see and fire at attackers.

The **Rumble Rocket** detaches from Knighton Castle and **blasts into orbit**. If the castle is under siege, the knights can get away **fast**.

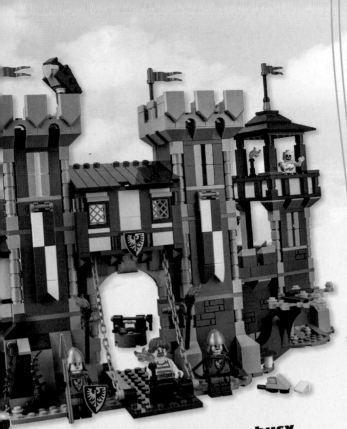

Ragana, the evil LEGO® Elves witch, is holding a Princess dragon egg captive in her **Magical Shadow Castle** (41180). Her fairytale castle is actually a nightmare, with **hidden traps** and a frightful **dungeon**.

Medieval castles were busy places. This one (31120) has a spinning water wheel, a prison, a blacksmith's, the king's room, a well, and a market place.

I keep the castle safe day and knight.

BUILDING CHALLENGE!

Can you build a working catapult or trebuchet from LEGO bricks?

As castle building developed and they became harder to attack, more **powerful weapons** were invented. One was the **trebuchet—a giant catapult.**

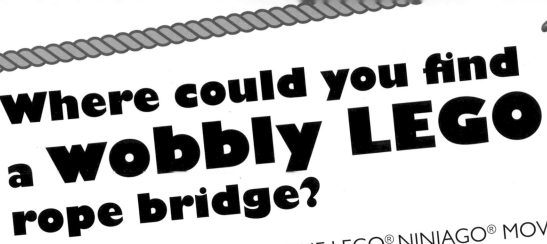

Where could you find a **wobbly LEGO** rope bridge?

Master Falls (70608) from THE LEGO® NINJAGO® MOVIE™ theme has a precarious rope bridge strung between two rocky jungle outcrops. Other LEGO sets have **arched** bridges, **suspension** bridges, **bascule** bridges, and even **famous** ones.

More than 500 years ago, the **Inca** civilization in South America used **rope bridges** to get across **canyons** and **gorges** in the Andes Mountains.

Jungle Garmadon controls the rope bridge. Can Wu and Kai defeat him or will they wind up in the suspended cage?

The **wobbly bridge** is snapped together with LEGO pieces originally created in gray for **caterpillar tracks**.

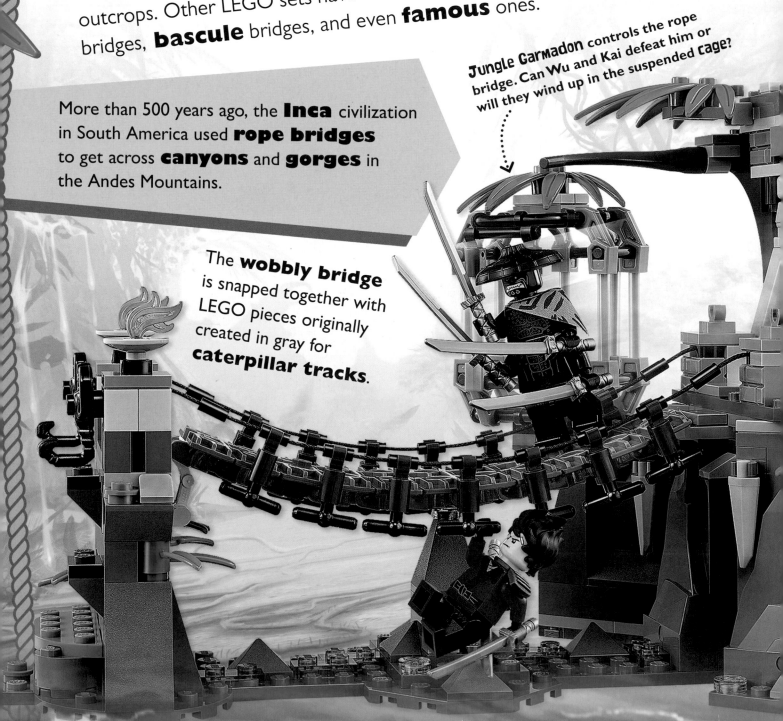

The stone, arched **Rialto Bridge** is the oldest bridge crossing the Grand Canal in **Venice**, Italy. In the LEGO model (21026), it stands with St. Mark's Basilica, St. Mark's Campanile and, far right, the **Bridge of Sighs**.

Venice

The **tallest bridge** in the world is the Millau Viaduct in France. At its tallest point, it is **1,125 ft** (343 m)—nearly **9,000** minifigures would have to stand on each others' heads to reach the top.

BUILDING CHALLENGE!

Build a LEGO bridge between two pieces of furniture. How many minifigures can it hold?

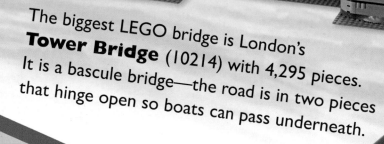

The biggest LEGO bridge is London's **Tower Bridge** (10214) with 4,295 pieces. It is a bascule bridge—the road is in two pieces that hinge open so boats can pass underneath.

I'll cross that bridge when I've built it.

The world's **longest bridge** is the Danyang–Kunshan Grand Bridge in China. It would take more than **5 million** 2x4 LEGO bricks just to lay a single line of them along the 102 mile- (164 km-) long bridge.

How many LEGO® bricks high is the Eiffel Tower?

The **Eiffel Tower** in Paris is approximately **33,750** LEGO bricks high and is 1,063 ft (324 m) tall. Its 2019 LEGO model (21044) is over 8 in (22 cm)—or just over 23 LEGO bricks tall. Many other LEGO® Architecture sets recreate tall, famous buildings.

The Eiffel Tower has **2,500,000** rivets (bolts)—and its LEGO counterpart has **321** LEGO pieces.

The **Elizabeth Tower** holds the **Big Ben** bell in the Palace of Westminster, which is home to the British Parliament.

20,000 lights **twinkle** on the **tower** at night for five minutes **every hour**, on the hour.

ELIZABETH TOWER
Location: London, UK
Date: Constructed 1843–1859
Height: 315 ft (96 m)
LEGO Set: 10253

Approx. **10,000** LEGO bricks high

FLATIRON BUILDING
Location: New York City
Date: Opened 1902
Height: 307 ft (93.5 m)
LEGO Set: 21023

Approx. **9,750** LEGO bricks high

Eiffel Tower
Location: Paris, France
Date: 1889
Height: 1,063 ft (324 m)

Approx. **33,750** LEGO bricks high

The triangular **Flatiron** building has stood at the **intersection** of Fifth Avenue and Broadway in New York City since 1902. At its narrowest point it's only 6 ft (1.83 m) across.

Flatiron Building

The race skyward has enabled cities to expand up as well as outward. Layers of transparent LEGO bricks look like stories of glass.

Aim high!

BUILDING CHALLENGE!

Can you estimate how many LEGO bricks tall your home is? Ask an adult to help estimate the building's height and measure a LEGO brick.

The Eiffel Tower has **1,665 steps!**

An Art Deco skyscraper, the **Empire State Building** opened in New York City in 1931. It was the first building in the world to have more than **100 stories.**

EMPIRE STATE BUILDING
Location: New York City
Date: Opened 1931
Height: 1,453 ft (443 m)
LEGO set: 21046

Approx. **46,150** LEGO bricks high

Paris's **Eiffel Tower** was created for the **World's Fair** in 1889 to mark the 100th anniversary of the French Revolution.

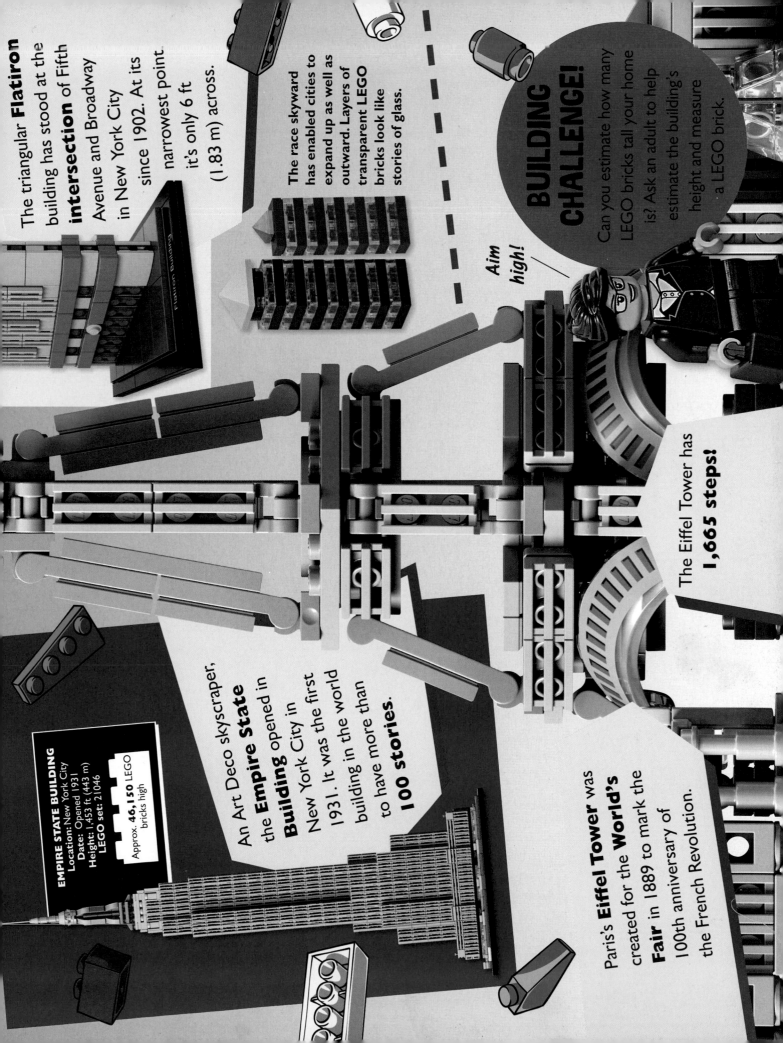

Which LEGO City hall boasts a golden statue?

The city hall in **Main Square** displays a **gleaming** golden statue over its door with a minifigure trophy and two claw pieces. The long-running LEGO® City theme includes many public buildings and **busy community workers** who keep our cities going, as well as a few who don't... like crooks.

Main Square (60271) features the busy metropolis and characters as seen in the **LEGO City Adventures** TV series.

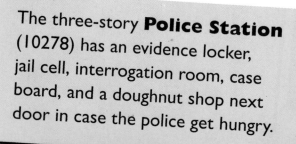

The three-story **Police Station** (10278) has an evidence locker, jail cell, interrogation room, case board, and a doughnut shop next door in case the police get hungry.

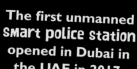

The first unmanned smart police station opened in Dubai in the UAE in 2017.

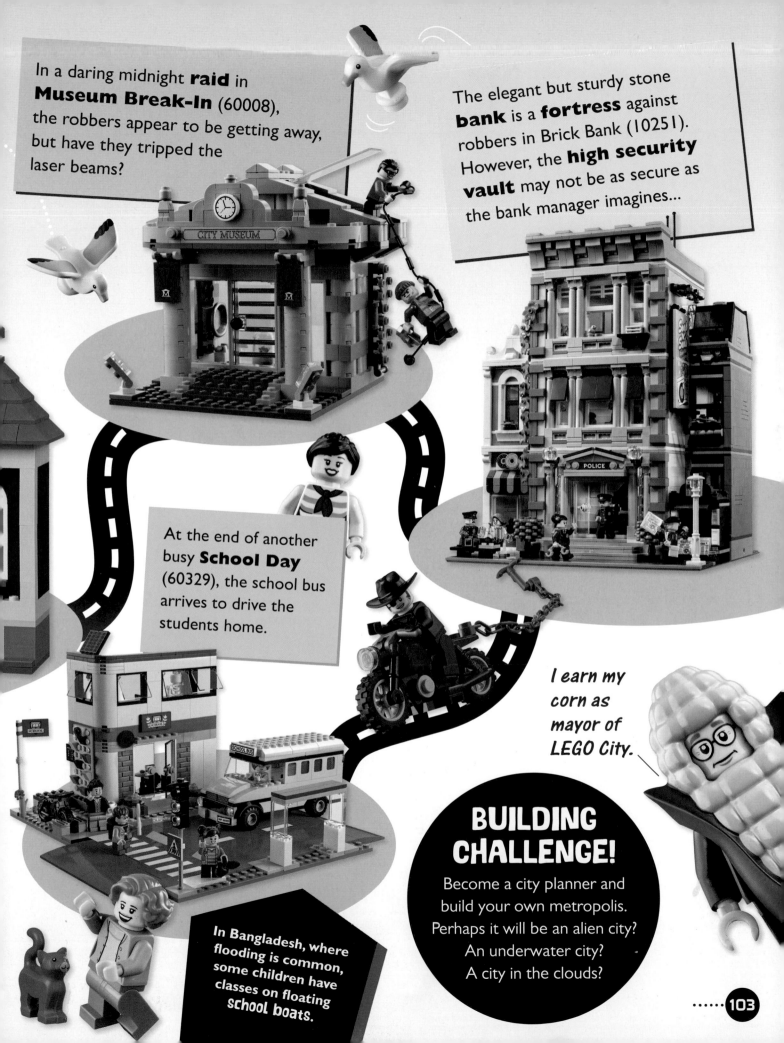

In a daring midnight **raid** in **Museum Break-In** (60008), the robbers appear to be getting away, but have they tripped the laser beams?

The elegant but sturdy stone **bank** is a **fortress** against robbers in Brick Bank (10251). However, the **high security vault** may not be as secure as the bank manager imagines...

At the end of another busy **School Day** (60329), the school bus arrives to drive the students home.

I earn my corn as mayor of LEGO City.

BUILDING CHALLENGE!

Become a city planner and build your own metropolis. Perhaps it will be an alien city? An underwater city? A city in the clouds?

In Bangladesh, where flooding is common, some children have classes on floating school boats.

This model (21037) has 774 bricks, but the real interactive **LEGO® House** visitor experience in Billund, Denmark, contains **25 million LEGO** bricks, including a **life-size** rainbow **waterfall**.

BUILDING CHALLENGE!

Why not build your dream home? What fantastical features would you add? A moat? A roller coaster? A secret laboratory?

Which LEGO house has a built-in skate ramp?

The **Modular Skate House** (31081) is a skater's dream home with its own built-in half-pipe, vertical ramp, and hand rails for **skateboarding** or **scooter tricks**. There are all kinds of different LEGO **houses**, each one perfectly designed for its LEGO minifigure residents!

The world's **biggest** gingerbread house was 60 ft (18.28 m) long, 42 ft (12.8 m) wide, and 10 ft (3.07 m) tall. In 2013, visitors in Texas could enter it and meet **Santa** to raise money for charity.

Home sweet home!

A gingerbread man's **gingerbread house** (60267) is his castle, and it's covered with tasty treats and festive snow. The transparent windows are colored like hard candies, and the fireplace has a light-up brick.

The skaters' house of fun also has **monkey bars**, a **climbing wall**, and a **basketball hoop**. The 3-in-1 set can be rebuilt as an **arcade** and **cafe** or a **skate park**.

For a UK TV show in 2009, more than 1,000 volunteers **built** a **life-size LEGO house** from **3.2 million** LEGO bricks. It had a flushing **toilet**, hot shower, **mood** lighting, and even a pair of LEGO slippers!

Medieval houses like Medieval Blacksmith (21325) were built with wooden frames and **wattle and daub**—latticed sticks covered in mud or clay—and a fireproof stone chimney. Brown **LEGO** tiles attach to sideways bricks to create the **frame** effect.

The Ferris Wheel stands **23 ½ in** (60 cm) **tall**.

This colorful set is built with **2,464** LEGO pieces.

The world's **First Ferris Wheel** was created by George **W. Ferris** and was displayed at the World's Columbian Exposition in Chicago in **1893**.

Gondolas are attached with LEGO® **Technic axles** so they stay **upright** as they revolve with the big wheel.

The **world's biggest** LEGO Ferris Wheel built by a fan is **11 ft 11 in** (3.64 m) tall. Inspired by the London Eye, the model uses **40,000 bricks** and rotates with a motor.

Which LEGO set is 360 degrees of fun?

The **Ferris Wheel (10247)** is the **biggest LEGO Ferris Wheel** set made by the LEGO Group, both by size and the number of bricks used. A crank **spins** the wheel through limitless **360** degree rotations and it can even be fitted with a LEGO Power Functions motor so it revolves automatically.

Let the good times roll!

LEGO **wheels**, held taut with elastic bands, keep the big wheel on track.

LEGO FERRIS WHEEL ROUND UP

Over 10 ½ in (27 cm) tall

Ferris Wheel (31119) – LEGO Creator 3-in-1

Over 15 in (38 cm) tall

Big Fair (10840) – LEGO DUPLO

Over 12 in (31 cm) tall

Amusement Park Roller Coaster (41130) – LEGO FRIENDS

Over 6 in (16 cm) tall

Fairground Carousel (31095) – LEGO Creator 3-in-1

BUILDING CHALLENGE!

How tall a tower can you build without it falling over?

The **scout tower** on the waterfront three-story Fire Station (60215) is used for monitoring scouting **drones** and dispatching the **fire-fighting** truck and water scooter.

The **airport** terminal in Passenger Airplane (60262) has a **control tower**. Glass walls and a spinning seat give great views to the air-traffic controller, and a **radar** bar helps them direct the planes.

The **tower** of the spooky **Haunted House** (10273) contains a spine-tingling ride. Minifigures are wound up to the top of the tower in a cart—then **freefall** to the bottom!

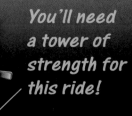

You'll need a tower of strength for this ride!

The **tallest** television transmission tower in the world is the Tokyo Skytree in Tokyo, Japan. It is 2,080 ft (634 m) high—taller than 16,600 **LEGO** antenna pieces.

Which tottering LEGO tower holds a ninja control center?

NINJAGO City Gardens (71741) is a five-tiered building with a ninja control room in the top of its tower for Lloyd, Kai, Zane, Cole, Jay, and Nya. There are LEGO towers in many architectural styles, each with a different purpose.

NINJAGO City Gardens has a mammoth 5,685 pieces, including a collectible golden Wu Legacy minifigure to celebrate the tenth anniversary of the LEGO NINJAGO theme.

New York

I carry a torch for America.

STATUE OF LIBERTY

Location: New York City, United States of America

Date: Officially opened 1886

Height: (Including base) 305 ft (92.99 m)

Lady Liberty stands in the harbor of New York City as a symbol of freedom and democracy. The statue was a gift to America from the people of France.

Green LEGO bricks re-create the color of **copper** that has turned **green** after **reacting** with **oxygen** in the air.

How many LEGO Statue of Liberty models would be as tall as the real thing?

It would take **212 LEGO** models of the **Statue of Liberty** (21042) stacked on top of each other to reach the top of the original monument. The set belongs to the LEGO **Architecture** theme, whose models are scaled mini-versions of real buildings and landmarks.

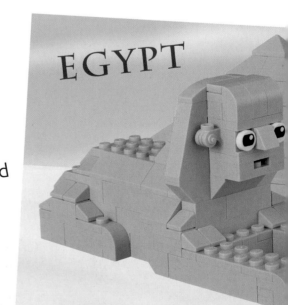

EGYPT

BUCKINGHAM PALACE
Location: London, United Kingdom
Date: Official royal residence since 1837
Width: 354 ft (108 m)
LEGO Set: 21029
Buckingham Palace is the official London residence of the Queen of the United Kingdom, Elizabeth II. The first monarch to live here was Queen Victoria.

LONDON

You would need more than **450 LEGO** sets piled up to reach the top of the actual **Arc de Triomphe** in Paris.

Paris

BUILDING CHALLENGE!
The Pyramids of Giza in Egypt are more than four thousand years old. Can you build a modern LEGO version in a different size and color?

ARC DE TRIOMPHE DE L'ETOILE
Location: Paris, France
Date: Officially opened 1836
Height: 164 ft (50 m)
LEGO Set: 21036
A symbol of France, the Arc de Triomphe was commissioned by Napoleon I in 1806 to mark the French army's victory at the Battle of Austerlitz in 1805.

GREAT SPHINX OF GIZA
Location: Egypt
Date: c. 2500 BCE
Height: 66 ft (20 m)
Length: 240 ft (73 m)
The enormous statue was carved from a single piece of limestone to guard the pyramid of Khafre at Giza. The pyramids were sacred burial places of the kings.

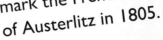

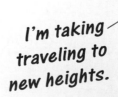

I'm taking traveling to new heights.

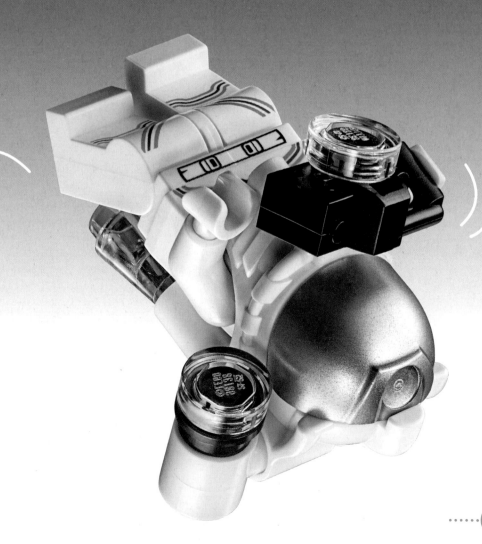

CHAPTER 5

Space
and
Adventure

How many minifigures would it take to reach the moon?

The moon is 238,855 miles 384,400 km from Earth. It would take about **9.6 billion** minifigures standing on top of each other to reach the same distance. That's **more minifigures than there are people on the planet!**

The surface of the **moon** is cold and dusty. It is covered in mountains and valleys, called **craters**, created

Earth

Humans leave trash everywhere they go!
Space junk is made up of parts of rockets, old satellites, and other things that astronauts have left behind on their missions.

BUILDING CHALLENGE!

Build the tallest tower you can, using your bricks and minifigures. Your tower may not reach the moon, but can it reach the ceiling?

The moon's low gravity makes walking on it difficult. The easiest way to get around is to jump like a kangaroo!

where space rocks have crashed into the moon!

So far, **LEGO®** bricks or minifigures (in various forms) have traveled to **Mars, Jupiter,** and the **International Space Station.**

Ciao from the moon!

12 astronauts have set foot on the moon. No minifigures have been there yet, but perhaps one day they will!

NASA helped plan and design the Apollo 11 Lunar Lander (10266), to make the LEGO model as similar as possible to the real lunar lander!

COULD YOU BUILD A LEGO TOWER TO REACH THE MOON?

Well, there are many challenges:

1 The weight of the LEGO bricks would crush the ones underneath.

2 A LEGO builder couldn't build beyond the Earth's atmosphere as there's no oxygen!

3 Space junk or space rocks might crash into the tower.

What's the tallest LEGO® rocket?

— *One day, I'm going to explore space!*

One of the **largest rockets** was NASA's **Saturn V**, part of the Apollo program that landed the first people on the moon in **1969**. So, of course, the **tallest** LEGO rocket is also the **Apollo Saturn V** (92176). The rocket is more than **1 m (3 ft 3 in) tall** and has **1,969 pieces.**

Apollo space shuttle and rescue rocket

SATURN V FACTS

» Saturn V was **110.6 m tall** (363 ft), taller than the Statue of Liberty.

» It weighed **3,268 tons** (2,965 metric tons) when fully fueled and ready to launch. That's about the same as **30 blue whales.**

» The first mission to land on the moon was called **Apollo 11.**

BUILDING CHALLENGE!

Get ready to blast off into space! Look at the shape of the models on these pages. What features does your rocket need? How many astronauts will it carry?

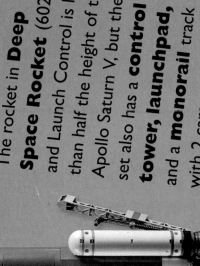

control tower

grappling arm

The rocket in **Deep Space Rocket** (60228) and Launch Control is less than half the height of the Apollo Saturn V, but the set also has a **control tower, launchpad,** and a **monorail** track with 2 cars.

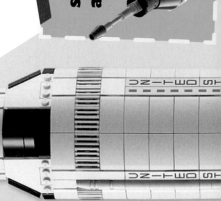

Set 31117 takes LEGO space **adventures** to a whole new level with the potential to build **3 great space vehicles—** a space shuttle, rocket, and lunar lander.

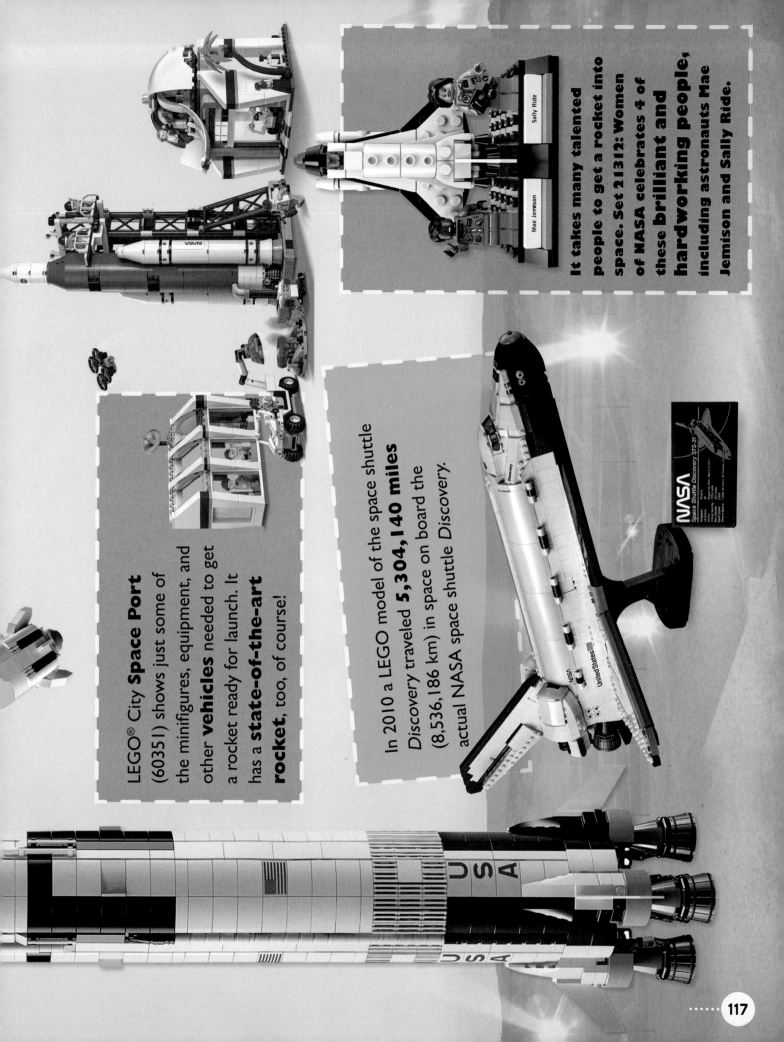

It takes many talented people to get a rocket into space. Set 21312: Women of NASA celebrates 4 of these **brilliant and hardworking people,** including astronauts Mae Jemison and Sally Ride.

Sally Ride

Mae Jemison

LEGO® City **Space Port** (60351) shows just some of the minifigures, equipment, and other **vehicles** needed to get a rocket ready for launch. It has a **state-of-the-art rocket,** too, of course!

In 2010 a LEGO model of the space shuttle *Discovery* traveled **5,304,140 miles** (8,536,186 km) in space on board the actual NASA space shuttle *Discovery.*

NASA
Space Shuttle Discovery STS-31

Which LEGO space station has a pizza oven?

Although there have been many awesome LEGO **space-themed sets** since the 1970s, there are only four official LEGO space stations. Amazingly, one of them, **Lunar Space Station** (60227), has a **pizza oven**! Well, it probably is a bit too far to order a takeout...

BUILDING CHALLENGE!

Design a space station: will you go big or keep things simple? How many astronauts will live there and what will they eat? Don't forget the solar panels, too.

Say cheese! Welcome to my home, it's space-cious.

A pizza oven is not the only **home comfort** in this set (60227). The 3 detachable modules can be put together in different ways and include a **treadmill**, anti-gravity **bed**, **TV** screen, and a kitchen. There's even a **plant**!

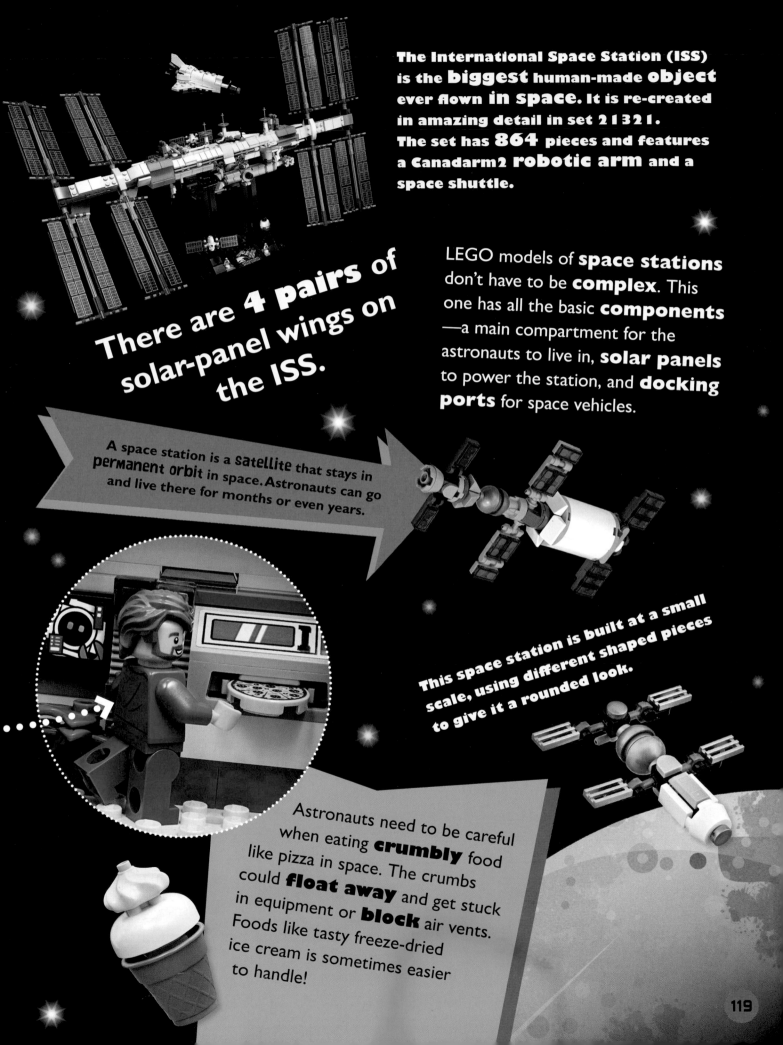

The International Space Station (ISS) is the **biggest** human-made **object** ever flown **in space**. It is re-created in amazing detail in set 21321. The set has **864** pieces and features a Canadarm2 **robotic arm** and a space shuttle.

There are **4 pairs** of solar-panel wings on the ISS.

LEGO models of **space stations** don't have to be **complex**. This one has all the basic **components** —a main compartment for the astronauts to live in, **solar panels** to power the station, and **docking ports** for space vehicles.

A space station is a **satellite** that stays in **permanent orbit** in space. Astronauts can go and live there for months or even years.

This space station is built at a small scale, using different shaped pieces to give it a rounded look.

Astronauts need to be careful when eating **crumbly** food like pizza in space. The crumbs could **float away** and get stuck in equipment or **block** air vents. Foods like tasty freeze-dried ice cream is sometimes easier to handle!

PERSONAL TRAINER

Set 60230

The **personal trainer** makes sure that the astronauts are fit and **healthy**. They will also have to work out in space to stay strong in **zero gravity**.

BOTANIST

Set 60230

The **botanist** is studying how **plants** might grow in space. She creates space-like conditions in her lab, and hopes to send some plants into **space** on the next shuttle.

MECHANICAL ENGINEER

Set 60230

The **mechanical engineer** designs and **checks** all the machines and **tools** that will be used on the space **mission**.

ROCKET ENGINEER

Set 60230

The **rocket engineer** is really good at **math**. She has to **calculate** all the weights, measurements, and angles to make sure the rocket can **take off** and land **safely**.

BUILDING CHALLENGE!

How many minifigures do you need for your next space mission? Assemble your team and build all the equipment they'll need, such as drones, computers, drills, support vehicles, and a cool command center.

Engineers are **scientists** who want to know **how and why** things work. They **design and build** complex machines, systems, tools, or structures.

DRONE ENGINEER

Set
60230

The **drone engineer** is perfecting a drone that will be able to **explore** areas of **space** that astronauts can't get to. She can control it from the command center back on **Earth**.

LAUNCH DIRECTOR AND TEAM

Set
60228

The **launch director** makes sure that the launch happens safely and on time. They work in the **control center** with a **team** of scientists and other **experts**.

Around **400,000** people were involved in NASA's **Apollo** program in the **1960s and '70s**. These included astronauts, mission controllers, ground crew, caterers, engineers, scientists, nurses, doctors, mathematicians, and programmers.

REPORTER AND CAMERA OPERATOR

Set
60230

Space exploration is big news! The reporter and camera operator make sure that all key events and discoveries are **recorded** **and reported**.

How many minifigures does it take to run a space mission?

It takes at least **14** minifigures (and a robot) to run a space mission. In LEGO® City Space Research and Development (60230), a drone engineer, **rocket engineer**, mechanical engineer, **botanist**, reporter, camera operator, personal trainer, **7 astronauts**, and a robot figure are all hard at work.

Can I help out with a mission? I brought my own wrench.

121

On which planet do LEGO explorers find crystals?

LEGO **astronauts** love exploring the **galaxy**, visiting other planets, conducting research, and making amazing **discoveries**. On a trip to **Mars**, they found some fascinating blue **crystals** (60226). Scientist minifigures back on Earth can't wait to study them.

This **space shuttle** looks a bit like a plane and is best for **short missions**, such as orbiting the Earth.

Some sets combine the best parts of what scientists know about space and of what we might imagine. With Space Shuttle Adventure (31117) you can build **3** amazing space vehicles.

The **lunar lander** is ideal for exploring planets or other celestial bodies. It has **4** bendable "legs" and a central cylinder to anchor it firmly to the surface.

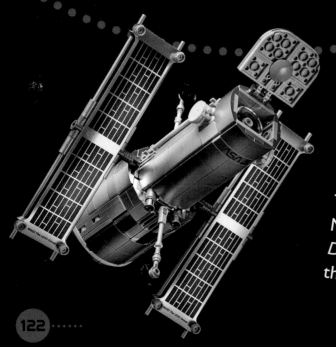

Scientists don't even need to travel to space to study it, thanks to the **Hubble Space Telescope**, re-created here (10283). The set also features the NASA **Space Shuttle** Discovery with payload doors that open to **launch** Hubble.

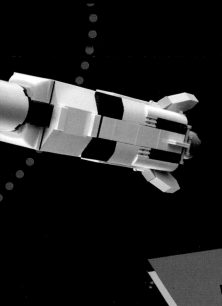

The **rocket** is taller and thinner than the space shuttle and is powerful enough to **zoom farther** into space.

Fancy a space party? Better planet!

Do aliens exist? No one knows. But many UAPs (Unidentified Aerial Phenomenons) have been officially documented, so something could be out there...

BUILDING CHALLENGE!

Create a rocket to blast into outer space, or a vehicle equipped to explore a planet. Build a friendly alien or two, and somewhere for your minifigures to hang out with them.

The mysterious **blue crystal** is safe inside a storage **drone**.

Whe.e would y--u find a LEGO woolly mammoth?

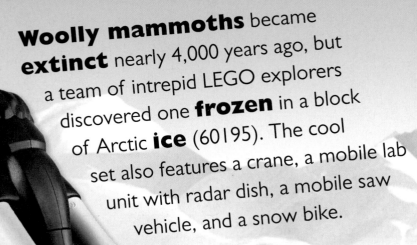

Woolly mammoths became **extinct** nearly 4,000 years ago, but a team of intrepid LEGO explorers discovered one **frozen** in a block of Arctic **ice** (60195). The cool set also features a crane, a mobile lab unit with radar dish, a mobile saw vehicle, and a snow bike.

WOOLLY MAMMOTH FACTS:

» Woolly mammoths are extinct relatives of **elephants**.

» They roamed the plains of North America, Europe, and Asia during the last Ice Age.

» They were about **10 ft** (3 m) tall and **13 ft** (4 m) long.

» Their long, curved tusks were about **13 ft** (4 m) long.

» Their bodies were covered in a layer of **fat** and thick, **shaggy** hair to keep them **warm**.

BUILDING CHALLENGE!

It's time for an Arctic adventure! Assemble your minifigure team and build a vehicle for them that can handle icy conditions. What will the team uncover— amazing animals, treasure, or maybe even aliens?

The Arctic subtheme of LEGO City also unearthed some other extinct animals preserved in ice. In Arctic Air Transport (60193), the team uses a **quadrocopter** to search the snowy terrain. They've found a **saber-toothed tiger!**

Another name for a saber-toothed tiger is a smilodon.

The claw gripper on the **ice crawler (60192)** is great for searching the ice and snow. The team has uncovered a **frozen rodent,** but need to take it back to the lab to find out more about it.

This **snowmobile** (60191) has skis and tracks to help it move over the ice and snow. The **husky dog** is part of the **team,** too. Huskies are very **intelligent** dogs and don't mind low temperatures.

Thankfully the explorers haven't found ME yet!

A combination of **tracks** and all-terrain **wheels** make this Arctic Scout Truck (60194) super steady even on icy ground. This time the team has found **a polar bear** in its ice cave and a **husky dog!**

Which LEGO villain keeps a fish tank in his volcano lair?

Lord **Garmadon** loves his **volcano** lair (70631). Most minifigures stay away from volcanoes in case they **erupt**, so it's the perfect hideaway to plan evil schemes against NINJAGO® City with his Shark Army. When he's not plotting, Garmadon likes to drink tea in his throne room and watch the **fish** in his **tank**.

Volcanoes **erupt** when **hot** liquid rock called **magma** escapes from deep inside the Earth through holes in the surface.

GIT AUTHORIZED ACCESS ONLY

BUILDING CHALLENGE!

Build a volcano in a circular shape. Don't forget to add some red and yellow bricks to show the lava flowing out! Then plan your adventure.

Why is that mountain making a rumbling sound?

The **drone** can fly above the volcano to **explore** areas that the minifigures cannot reach.

LEGO scientists love to **study** volcanoes. **Volcanologists** want to learn more about how and why they erupt and the **geologists** study the volcanic rocks. They use specialized **vehicles** and **equipment** to help them.

When magma reaches the surface of the Earth it is called **lava**.

Alpaca Mountain (41432) is home to many plants and animals, but the volcano may erupt at any moment. **LEGO® FRIENDS** have a **zip line**, canoe, and a **rescue** helicopter ready to rescue any animals in **danger**.

The Volcano Starter Set (60120) is packed with volcano-themed play potential. There's a **volcano** with an eruption function; a boulder with a **crystal** inside; an **ATV** with a walkie-talkie; plus a camera, ax, and a metal detector.

Snap! The jungle explorer swings right by the croc. Phew! That was close.

BUILDING CHALLENGE!

Create a jungle scene with lots of plants and other natural features. Try adding hiding places for some jungle creatures—perhaps a cave, a waterfall, rock, or even a secret stash of treasure.

What scary surprise lurks under a LEGO waterfall?

In Jungle Mobile Lab (60160) **4** brave minifigures are on a mission to explore and study the **jungle**. The set features a cool mobile lab, a kayak, a temple with treasure, a hungry **venus flytrap plant**, and a waterfall concealing a very scary surprise—a **crocodile**!

The **red spider** lurking in Jungle Cargo Helicopter (60158) appears in **8** sets. But there are actually nearly **3 million** spiders for every 1 human on the planet. Most are completely harmless, but it's still a little creepy...

If the spider doesn't scare them, this **panther** might! It wants a **bite** of the explorer's chicken **drumstick...**

Something much **smaller** than a crocodile lurks in Jungle Halftrack Mission (60159). If the jungle explorers move the stone inside the temple, they'll release a scary **spider!**

Jungles are usually found in **tropical** areas—places that are warm all year with plenty of rain.

The **7 minifigures** in Jungle Exploration Site (60161) are nearly outnumbered by jungle creatures. There's a **leopard**, crocodile, **snake**, frog, and 2 spiders waiting to greet the jungle visitors.

The minifigures are prepared for anything. They have **5** cool **vehicles** including this observation **truck**, which is carrying a **kayak** and a **motorcycle**.

An adult male tiger can travel **33 ft (10 m)** in a single **leap**. That's the equivalent of **13** footsteps from a human **man**.

Let me take a closer look at that...

A tiger lurks in Jungle Air Drop Helicopter (60162), but are the **minifigures** too busy setting up camp to **notice?**

Which swashbuckling minifigures sail the seas?

LEGO fans of all ages **love pirates**. That's why **swashbuckling** pirate minifigures have featured across many different themes. LEGO Creator set (31109) features a cool **pirate ship** and three pirate minifigures.

There is also a dedicated LEGO® **Pirates** theme. Since launching in 1989, more than **80** sets have been released. Pirates Chess (40158) pits pirates against Bluecoat soldiers and contains a whopping **20** minifigures.

Pirate Ship is a Creator **3-in-1 set** and can be rebuilt as a cozy **Pirates' Inn**, where pirates can go and relax, or a mysterious **Skull Island** with a spooky skeleton figure.

With **2,542** pieces, Pirates of Barracuda Bay (21322) might be the **ultimate** LEGO pirate model. It can be built as a **shipwreck island** or a **pirate ship** and features **8** minifigures, which are all exclusive to the set.

There are also **2 skeleton figures**, including a **one-legged pirate** skeleton!

Pirate ships don't need to be big builds. This simple mini model (11009) is tons of pirate fun and also becomes a **shadow puppet** when used with the Light Brick Shadow Casters.

The young pirates in Tree House Treasures (31078) have turned their ship into a cool tree house. It's great for storing treasure, but not very seaworthy!

Captain Redbeard and his crew, released in 1989, were the first minifigures to have **extra facial details**. Previous minifigures only had the classic LEGO smile.

Where did I leave my ship?

Which deep sea divers find a LEGO shipwreck full of gold bars?

LEGO minifigures love to **explore** and few places are more exciting and mysterious than the **ocean**. In Deep Sea Exploration Vessel (60095), a team of **7 divers** discover a shipwreck with a cargo of **gold bars**. Who does this treasure belong to, or is it a case of "finders keepers?"

BUILDING CHALLENGE!

Build a vessel to explore the ocean. Will it dive down to the depths or be equipped to study ocean life. What creatures might you find on your adventures?

The first deep-ocean dive took place in August **1934.**

Watch out for the **shark** and **octopus lurking** around the shipwreck. The team are here to **study** the ocean, not become a **tasty sea snack**!

Oceans cover 70 percent of the Earth's surface.

Has anyone seen a ship full of gold? I lost mine.

The LEGO divers sail the ocean in this **exploration vessel**. It has all the **equipment** they need, including a working winch with cage, a large **bridge** (the command center or cockpit of a ship), below-deck cabins, and a **lifeboat**.

E-06

EXPLORER-6

The divers also use **submarines** to explore the darkest **depths** of the ocean. The exploration sub can be winched down from the main ship, while the smaller sub is **controlled remotely**.

E-04

The **scuba scooter** is perfect for **shorter underwater** missions when the divers want to move **faster** and use less oxygen.

Ships could also use a small underwater **drone** to explore places that the minifigures can't reach.

CHAPTER 6

Minifigures

In space, there is **zero gravity**. That's why space toilets have footholds to stop astronauts from floating away. They work by suction to stop anything else from drifting off!

BUILDING CHALLENGE!

Build a toilet for a minifigure. Make sure it has a nice, comfy, round seat. What elements can you use? How about a life preserver?

Where do minifigures go to the toilet?

You'll be relieved to hear that LEGO® minifigures have lots of places to go to the bathroom. But they don't always go for the obvious reasons. In City Police Station (60047) a **crook escapes** through a **secret trapdoor** he has made under the prison toilets. He probably feels a bit drained by the time he emerges.

In South Korea there is a toilet **theme park**! It includes a toilet-shaped **house** built by the president of the World Toilet Association, which works to improve sanitation around the world.

The toilet in the detective's office is very old—the clue is the high cistern with **pull chain**. Modern toilets have low cisterns and handles or buttons to **flush**.

A MINIFIGURE ON THE GO NEEDS SOMEWHERE TO "GO." NO PROBLEM!

By the age of 80, the average person has spent more than **a year** of their life on the toilet!

These friends love the outdoor life, but not an **outdoor toilet**. Their forest house has a downstairs bathroom.

Forest House (41679)
– LEGO FRIENDS

Builders use a **portable toilet** while a building is being constructed. It will be a while before the plumbing is in!

Downtown Fire Brigade (60216)
– LEGO City

Another blockage? My plunger will sort that out!

The Gingerbread couple aren't happy if guests leave **chocolate drops** in their nice clean toilet.

Gingerbread House (10267)
– LEGO Creator Expert

This party's really popping!

Pea Pod Costume Girl Series 20 (71027)

Brick Costume Boy Series 20 (71027)

I'm a real party animal!

Llama Costume Girl Series 20 (71027)

Bear Costume Guy Series 19 (71025)

Pug Costume Guy Series 21 (71029)

Which minifigures wear the coolest costumes?

Elephant Costume Girl Series 18 (71021)

The Collectible LEGO Minifigure Series are among the coolest costume candidates. But who is coolest of the cool at this costume **party**? Well, it could be **Elephant Costume Girl**, or cheerful **Corn Cob Guy**, or the **Cute Little Devil**—you decide!

Unicorn Girl
Series 13 (71008)

Cowboy
Costume Guy
Series 18 (71021)

Wish I had some kitten heels...

Piggy Guy
Series 12 (71007)

Cat Costume Girl
Series 18 (71021)

Spider Suit Boy
Series 18 (71021)

BUILDING CHALLENGE!

Pick a minifigure and give them a hat. Then start adding more and more accessories. How many can you fit on before your minifigure topples over?

Unicorn Guy
Series 18 (71021)

At the annual **Carnevale** in Venice, people dress up in extravagant costumes inspired by clothes worn by Italian nobles from the 1500s to the 1700s. Fancy **masks** are a must!

I got mine at the costume imp-orium!

Banana
Guy
Series 16 (71013)

Do you think there will be food at this party? Oh, wait...

Cute
Little Devil
Series 16 (71013)

Corn Cob
Guy
Series 17 (71018)

Pizza Costume Guy
Series 19 (71025)

139

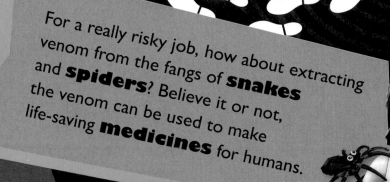

For a really risky job, how about extracting venom from the fangs of **snakes** and **spiders**? Believe it or not, the venom can be used to make life-saving **medicines** for humans.

It's a risky job but somebody has to do it.

Which minifigure has the most extreme job?

The **Spy** from Collectible LEGO Minifigure Series 16—aka **Agent A**—is a top contender. Extreme espionage is his game, and **infiltrating** evil organizations is his specialty. The undercover agent has freed **brainwashed** drones, **blown up** volcano lairs, and outwitted alien **Buggoids**. What's he up to now? Nobody knows!

The Ice Queen operates in extreme weather conditions. She reigns over a frosty kingdom where everything is made of ice. That includes horses, bread, and even **fire**. The collectible queen is part of Series 16.

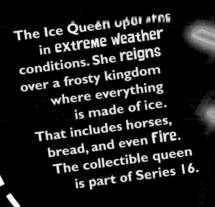

BUILDING CHALLENGE!

Give your favorite minifigure a new, extreme job. Stack two columns of 1x1 bricks under their feet and turn them into a daring circus stilt walker.

The engine revs… the crowd gasps… the LEGO **stunt biker** fearlessly launches his motorcycle off the **fiery ramp**. He's part of Stunt Team (60255). Will he land safely? It's all up in the air for now…

Stunt riders are always seeking more extreme **stunts** to try. In 2019, Marco George from the UK broke the record for the fastest speed while doing a **headstand** on a motorcycle. He reached 76.17 mph (122.59 km/h).

The pistol-packing **Highwayman** from Series 17 makes a living by robbing other minifigures. Real highwaymen were a menace to travelers in the **1600s** and **1700s**.

WANTED
BUILT or BROKEN
REWARD
$300,000,000

From Series 19 comes the **Galactic Bounty Hunter**. He's swooping through space **hunting down**… well, whomever he's paid to hunt down. Good guys? Bad guys? It's all the same to him as long as he gets his **reward!**

The world record for a javelin throw is 310 ft (94.48 m). That's as long as **2,462** minifigures laid end to end!

Next thing I'm throwing is a party to celebrate my win!

Athlete
Series 20 (71027)

The medals at the **2020** Tokyo Olympics were made from **recycled** metals such as those used in **smartphones**.

How many LEGO® athletes have won gold medals?

Eleven minifigures have gone for gold—and won! The **Athlete** from **Collectible** LEGO Minifigure **Series 20** is among them. She's a whiz with the **javelin** and a dazzler with the **discus**. In fact, there's no **throwing** event this plastic powerhouse won't throw herself into. Give the golden girl a cheer!

Why do athletes bite their gold medals?

Up until **1912** the medals were **solid** gold. Gold dents easily, so teeth marks proved the medal was **genuine**. Modern medals only have to contain 0.2 oz (6 g) gold, but the tradition remains.

We call games played on snow or ice **winter sports**. They include ice hockey, ski jumping, bobsled, and skating. **Skiing** and **snowboarding** are among the most popular, especially with these minifigures from City Ski Resort (60203).

Chemicals in pool water can make the eyes sting, so swimmers wear **goggles** to protect them. This **Swimming Champion** from Series 7 can remove hers with a turn of her head.

BUILDING CHALLENGE!

Stack tiles to make a 3-level podium for minifigure athletes. The gold level should be in the center, silver on the left, and bronze on the right.

Who's got the wickedest wheels? LEGO® City Skate Park (60290) has three contenders—a **BMX** rider, a **skateboarder**, and a high-flying **wheelchair** athlete. The set comes with pipes, ramps, and grind rails, but you could use whatever pieces you have to build an arena for wheel-riding minifigures.

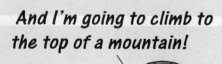

These minifigures haven't won a prize, but that's OK. They're all part of a Collectible series, so they are the prize!

Yay! Go us!

We're at the top of our game!

And I'm going to climb to the top of a mountain!

Rugby Player
Series 19 (71025)

Kickboxer
Series 16
(71013)

Fencer
Series 13 (71008)

Martial Arts Boy
Series 20
(71027)

Mountain Biker
Series 19 (71025)

Mountain Climber
Series 11 (71002)

Do aliens really exist?

Scientists think they might. They're using **radio telescopes** to look for **signals** from intelligent life forms out in space.

BUILDING CHALLENGE!

Build your alien minifigures a UFO landing pad. Use a round base plate and add colored tiles to form a weird alien symbol.

Another word for aliens is "extraterrestrials." It's made up of two parts: "extra" means "outside" and "terrestrial" means "of the Earth."

In **1947** a mysterious flying object **crashed** on a ranch in Roswell, New Mexico. People were excited—could this be an alien craft? Only in **1994** did the US military reveal that it was a top-secret US **spy balloon**.

This rocket-riding minifigure should be on the **alert** for **space hijackers**. If their UFO breaks down, an alien will take any transportation they can get!

Welcome, aliens! We know you come in peace!

Where might you spot an alien minifigure?

Peek inside a LEGO **UFO** and you'll see an alien at the controls. Aliens know the space lanes like the back of their hands (or tentacles), and this one (left) from LEGO® Alien Conquest Earth Defense (7066) has already landed on our planet. Look out, **Earth**!

Aliens might resemble jellyfish, sausages, flowers—anything, really. It would depend on **conditions** on their planet. When you're building a LEGO alien, be as **imaginative** as you like. These LEGO aliens have **plant pieces** for tentacles and **flippers** for feet.

Stop hassling us!

We're innocent tourists

| Alien Android LEGO Alien Conquest (7066) | Cyber Drone LEGO Creator 3-in-1 (31111) | Classic Alien Series 6 (8827) | Alien Series 21 (71029) | Galaxy Trooper Series 13 (71008) |

But do they come in peace? If not, the **Space Police Guy** could have a planet-size riot on his hands!

Space Police Guy
Series 21 (71029)

Who was the first LEGO minifigure?

The very **first minifigure** was a **police officer** in **1978**. He appeared in five sets that year. Minifigures today follow the same design with three basic parts: a head, a torso with movable arms and hands, and a piece with hips and movable legs.

I'm known as Bobby.

Minifigure hands can grip, which has led to the development of many accessories over the decades.

Since the launch of the minifigure in **1978**, an estimated **9 billion** minifigures have been created. That's enough to circle Earth's equator more than **5 and a half** times!

TOP 5 LEGO SETS WITH THE MOST MINIFIGURES

1 LEGO® Castle Giant Chess Set
(852293)—2008—**31** minifigures

2 LEGO Kingdoms Chess Set
(853373)—2012—**28** minifigures

3 LEGO® Marvel Daily Bugle
(76178)—2021—**25** minifigures

4 LEGO KNIGHTS' KINGDOM Chess
(851499)—2005—**24** minifigures

5 LEGO® Star Wars™ Death Star
(75159)—2016—**23** minifigures

HOW TALL IS A LEGO PERSON?

Proportioned just like minifigures, tiny **nanofigures** were first created as trophies. Some named characters are printed and appear in mini-scale sets.

» **HEIGHT: 1 ½ bricks**

Introduced in 2009 as playing pieces for LEGO games, **microfigures** are simplified characters.

» **HEIGHT: 2 bricks**

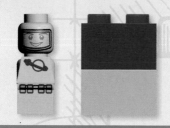

11 variants of the **baby** have been introduced since 2016.

» **HEIGHT: 2 bricks**

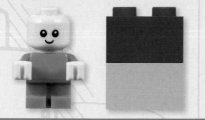

Many LEGO children have a **short leg** piece, which was introduced in 2002 for the *Star Wars* Character, Yoda.

» **HEIGHT (without hair): 3 bricks and 1 plate tall**

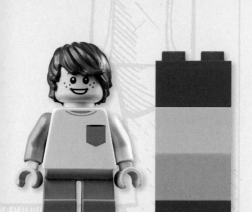

An articulated **medium-size leg** piece was first used for teenage wizards and witches in the LEGO® Harry Potter™ theme in 2018.

» **HEIGHT (without hair): 3 bricks and 2 plates tall**

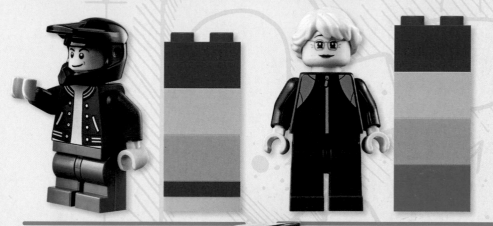

The **classic minifigure** elements designed in 1978 are the same today. Alternatives with sloped and curved skirt pieces are the same height.

» **HEIGHT (without hair): 4 bricks tall**

The **mini doll** figure was first created for the LEGO® FRIENDS theme in 2012, but has since expanded to other LEGO sets.

» **HEIGHT (without hair, to top of stud): 4 bricks and 2 plates tall**

A regular minifigure on **stilts** stands on two 1x1x3 bricks in People Pack Fun Fair (60234) in 2019.

» **HEIGHT (without hair): 7 bricks tall**

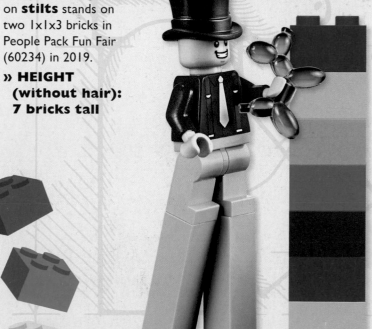

147

Why are ghosts so bad at lying?

Because you can see right through them.

The Collectible LEGO Minifigure Series 14 is full of **frightful fiends** and **foes**, including a **Zombie Cheerleader, Banshee, Zombie Pirate,** and a **Wacky Witch.**

Some parts of the world celebrate **Halloween** on **October 31** with **dressing up** and **trick or treating**. The roots of the tradition go back more than **two thousand years**.

Which spooky minifigure has two heads?

Scott Francis has been **gloomied**! He's been **possessed** by a ghost in the LEGO® Hidden Side theme and has become a two-headed cross between a **ghost** and a **zombie**. His minifigure is one of many ghoulish and ghastly LEGO builds that go bump in the night.

Scott's **gloombie** form in Jack's Beach Buggy (**70428**) has regular minifigure pieces plus an extra **fluorescent** neck brace for his **extra head.**

BUILDING CHALLENGE!

What kind of spooky creature can you build? How monstrous can you make it?

Who lives in a house like this? Do **you dare** knock on the door and find out?

A LEGO app makes sets come **alive** and **reveals** the **Hidden Side** for **ghost-hunting** adventures aboard **Captain Jack's Wrecked Shrimp Boat (70419).**

The hooded **ghost** and top-hatted **skeleton** are part of the spine-chilling and spine-jolting fairground ride **Haunted House** (10273).

I wouldn't be seen dead without my hat.

The ripped sails of **bony** green and white leg pieces are whipped up in the storm as the **ghostly galleon** sails the seven sinister seas.

Which LEGO monster minifigure hides in a snowy lair?

BUILDING CHALLENGE!

Build some tiny trolls—you'll only need a few bricks. They'll want a home, so next build a bridge for them to hide under, using arch pieces.

The LEGO minifigure **Yeti** has white fur, so it's well **camouflaged** in its snowy lair. Why is it hiding? Is it waiting to leap out and make a snack of passing minifigures? Not this one from Collectible LEGO Minifigure **Series 11**. It clearly prefers to chill out with an **ice pop!**

Just a few bricks can create a **cool LEGO monster!** This wandering **giant** has **long legs** thanks to stacked 1 x 1 bricks, and a **club** with **studs** on the side.

Yetis are big, shaggy, humanlike creatures said to live in the mountains of Nepal. It's likely that sightings of yetis are really of bears.

MEET THE MONSTERS

The Monster Scientist has a lot of brain room. He'll need it if he hopes to remember all the monster minifigures that have appeared since Zombie in Series 1. Here are a few of them.

Minotaur
Series 6 (8827)

If this bull-head invites you to their a-maze-ing home… don't go!

Gargoyle enjoys stunning views from his cathedral penthouse.

Specter
Series 14 (71010)

A spect-acular dungeon is where spooky Specter likes to haunt.

Fly Monster
Series 13 (71008)

Gargoyle
Series 14 (71010)

A cozy cow pie to settle down in is all Fly Monster asks.

Is the **Wolf Guy** from Collectible Series 14 really a **Werewolf**, or just a dude in costume? Check out the night sky, because most werewolves only come out at the **full moon**. A-woooo!

There's a name for the study of mysterious creatures not proven to exist: **cryptozoology**.

The **Cyclops** minifigure (Series 9) and **Lady Cyclops** (Series 13) just don't see **eye to eye**. They never agree whose turn it is to sweep up the bricks.

The more monsters the merrier, right?

Different LEGO monsters need different homes. Any marine monster would love to bed down in this **seabed** nook, with softly waving weeds made from **vine pieces**.

Lunar New Year festival begins with the **first new moon** of the lunar calendar and ends 15 days later on the **first full moon**.

Splash! Friends Stephanie, Emma, and Olivia are riding some **epic** slides at the **waterpark**!

I'm looking for buried treasure!

Happy New Year! This minifigure is having a great time at a **lantern festival** to celebrate Lunar New Year.

Zoom! Mia loves to pedal her **paddleboat**, while Andrea rides the waves on her **surfboard**. The **beach house** is the perfect vacation spot!

Gotcha! **Winter** vacations are super **fun** for these minifigures. **Snowball fights** are the best!

My family visits a carnival every year. It's awesome!

BUILDING CHALLENGE!

Build a dream vacation destination for your minifigures. Is it a beach scene, a campsite, or a winter wonderland?

National or public holidays are days when most people don't have to work or go to school. **Argentina** has the most national holidays with **19 per year**.

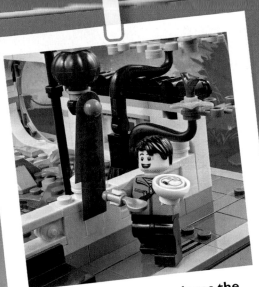

Yum! This minifigure loves the sweet Tang Yuan **dumplings** that are served during the Lantern Festival. More please!

Relaxing by a **pool** with a delicious **ice cream cone** is this minifigure's idea of the **perfect** vacation.

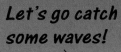

Let's go catch some waves!

All aboard! Awesome treats like this winter **train ride** make the holidays **extra special**.

This family has all the **comforts** of home in their camper but can get closer to **nature**.

How do minifigures spend their **vacations?**

Everyone needs a **vacation** sometimes, including the LEGO minifigures. Some minifigures like to take time out and **relax** at the beach, while others prefer nature **adventures** or exploring new places. One thing's certain, minifigures know how to have **fun**! Check out these minifigure vacation snaps.

Ski vacations are my favorite!

I have to think quickly to save my patients.

Which minifigures save the day?

The number of **LEGO minifigures** in the world is growing all the time, and they're a **talented** bunch! They do every job, from actor to zookeeper, and everything in between. However, when **disaster** strikes or **emergencies** happen, it's minifigures like these who'll race to **save** the day.

These **medically trained** minifigures are experts in bumps, bruises, and every kind of illness. If a minifigure gets sick or hurt, they'll get to them as **fast** as they can.

The **first** known police-like organization was in Ancient Egypt, in about **3000 BCE**.

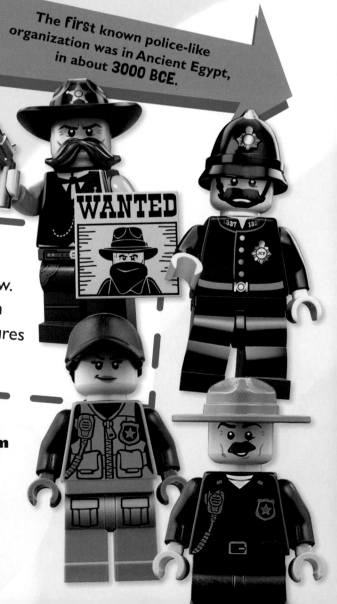

WANTED

Crooks beware! These **brave** minifigures are here to uphold the law. They're **trained** to find clues, catch criminals, and make sure that minifigures can live **safely** and peacefully.

The police use many **awesome** vehicles, from fast cars to state-of-the-art helicopters. This **motorcycle** can zoom past any traffic jams to get to the crime scene.

Firefighters have to be very **fit** and **strong** and they always work as a **team**.

If a fire breaks out, these **firefighter** minifigures don't hesitate. The **fire engine** is on standby at all times, with all the firefighting equipment **checked** and **ready** to go. That fire will be out in no time!

With **sirens** blaring, the fire engine races to save the day. The **ladder** extends to reach any trapped minifigures, and the **hose** is ready to spray water on the flames.

Firefighters also help minifigures who are **trapped**, or cats who get **stuck** in trees.

If anyone's in trouble, I just dive right in.

If a minifigure gets into **trouble** at sea, the lifeboat crew will **race** to the rescue.

I keep minifigures safe when they're swimming.

I'm ready to fly to the rescue.

I patrol the ocean.

I save the day, too —I help animals.

BUILDING CHALLENGE!

Emergency! Many, many minifigures need saving. Can you assemble a team to help them all? What vehicles and equipment do they need?

Index

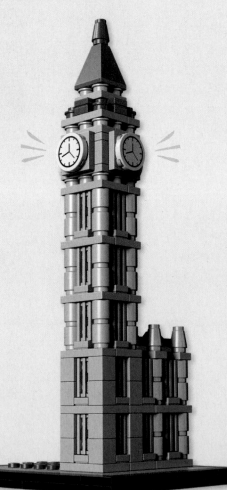

Playing hide-and-seek? I'll find you in ICU!

Penguin Random House

Senior Editors Ruth Amos and Elizabeth Cook
Senior US Editor Megan Douglass
Editor Nicole Reynolds
Senior Designer Anne Sharples
Designers Thelma Jane Robb, Lisa Sodeau,
and James McKeag
Production Editor Siu Yin Chan
Senior Production Controller Lloyd Robertson
Managing Editor Paula Regan
Managing Art Editor Jo Connor
Publishing Director Mark Searle

Written by Elizabeth Dowett, Julia March and Catherine Saunders
Nature Consultant Cathriona Hickey
Space Consultant Giles Sparrow
Additional models designed and created by Emily Corl,
Rod Gillies, Kevin Hall, Simon Pickard

DK would like to thank the following for their kind permission
in allowing us to use their images in this edition: Disney Enterprises,
NASA and Warner Bros.

DK would also like to thank Randi Sørensen, Tess Howarth, Heidi K. Jensen,
Paul Hansford, and Martin Leighton Lindhart at the LEGO Group; and Vanessa
Bird for proofreading and index creation.

First American Edition 2022
Published in the United States by DK Publishing
1450 Broadway, Suite 801, New York, NY 10018

Page design copyright © 2022 Dorling Kindersley Limited
DK, a Division of Penguin Random House LLC
22 23 24 25 26 10 9 8 7 6 5 4 3 2 1
001–326321–May/2022

A catalog record for this book
is available from the Library of Congress.
ISBN 978-0-7440-5034-9

DK books are available at special discounts when purchased
in bulk for sales promotions, premiums, fund-raising, or educational use.
For details, contact: DK Publishing Special Markets,
1450 Broadway, Suite 801, New York, NY 10018
SpecialSales@dk.com

Printed and bound in China
For the curious
www.dk.com
www.LEGO.com

This book was made with Forest Stewardship
Council ™ certified paper—one small step in
DK's commitment to a sustainable future.
For more information go to
www.dk.com/our-green-pledge